IMAGES
of our
INHERITANCE

IMAGES
of our
INHERITANCE

James Sidney & Sarah Stewart

WHITECAP BOOKS

Vancouver / Toronto / New York

Edited by Elaine Jones
Proofread by Elizabeth McLean
Cover design by Jennifer Conroy
Interior design by Tanya Lloyd
Printed on recycled paper in Canada by Friesens Printing

CANADIAN CATALOGUING IN PUBLICATION DATA

Sidney, James, 1972–
    Images of our inheritance

    Includes index.
    ISBN 1-55110-944-1

    1. Endangered ecosystems—Canada. 2. Sidney, James, 1972– —Journeys—Canada.
3. Stewart, Sarah, 1972– —Journeys—Canada. I. Stewart, Sarah, 1972– II. Title.
QH77.C3S52 1999   577.1'0971   C99-910845-X

The publisher acknowledges the support of the Canada Council for the Arts and the Cultural Services Branch of the Government of British Columbia for our publishing program. We acknowledge the financial support of the Government of Canada through the Book Industry Development Program for our publishing activities.

For our parents.

CONTENTS

FOREWORD

This is a story — a true one — of Earth, of Canada, and of two young people who represent the best hope of our future. It is a story not of what can be, but of what must be — the story for the new millennium.

Sarah Stewart and James Sidney have a personal commitment to the health and well-being of the biosphere. They do not separate what they know from what they feel, and they know a lot and feel it strongly. This is an "intelligent" and "caring" book, full of sensitive images and well-chosen words.

This book is not a diatribe against business, land developers and car-polluting suburbanites, eco-freaks, or anybody else. Rather, it is a reasonable, holistic assessment of where we go wrong, and how we must change — or will be forced to change. Sarah and James speak of the rich inheritance from which we have separated ourselves physically and spiritually, conscious of the fact that we cannot care for what we have not met or love what we do not know.

Our distant ancestors knew only a small territory. Our recent ancestors knew a valley, an island, or a range of sand dunes. Our grandparents and, especially, our parents travelled farther afield, aware even of continents. Each in turn developed some sense of responsibility for the area they knew. But we, who have an overview of the entire planet, are the biosphere in the process of understanding itself. Or we should be. This is the task that James and Sarah take so seriously.

In their hard-nosed, but often gentle prose, James and Sarah show us ways, including easy ways, to begin to reconnect with Earth's environments, its communities large and small. They assume the obvious — that we will function as a whole community or we will not function at all — and in sharing their personal experiences of being with nature, they make us want to join them.

— Freeman Patterson

ACKNOWLEDGEMENTS

This book began as an aspiration, a dream. The following people were instrumental in its realization.

We'd like to start by thanking our close family and friends for their continued support during the years it took to produce this volume. Especially, we'd like to acknowledge Dennis and Dianne Stewart, without whom the project would never have gotten underway.

Apart from sharing his valuable time and wisdom, we'd like to thank Freeman Patterson for his unfailing belief in us. In one sense, he represents our best hopes for the future. Perhaps one day we can mature into such genuine and generous spirits.

Not only was it an inspiration to spend five weeks with two of Canada's premier artists, it kept us from packing up and heading home from the start. Without Kathy and John Hooper's remarkable generosity, hospitality, and home-baked bread, we could never have made it through the first month away from home.

We are also indebted to the membership of the Tsuruoka Karate Federation. Countrywide, we could count on a hot meal, a cold beer, and a dry place to sleep. They treated us like family and embodied the best of the martial spirit. OSU!

Barbara Stokes and Gordon Sauvé helped with preliminary planning and editing. Their expertise, good humour and friendship is much appreciated.

Susan Kiil graciously shared her knowledge of publishing during initial planning, helping fine-tune the theme of the project.

Many staff at the Canadian Parks and Wilderness Society, World Wildlife Fund Canada, Carolinian Canada, and the Western Canada Wilderness Committee provided information and support during our travels. We want to thank them just for existing, and we want to encourage everyone to support them.

Also, we'd like to thank Trans North Helicopters of Dawson City for our flight into the Tombstone Mountains.

BEGINNINGS

Hampton Marsh

It was to be a story about pictures, about new attitudes, about the next generation. We decided to start on the east coast of Canada, where the new day first begins. It was also to be a story about photographs and about perceptions, so it was appropriate that we chose the province where Canada's most senior and respected landscape photographer, Freeman Patterson, lives.

"So where's your first location?" asked Freeman.

I squeezed the phone till my knuckles turned white and tried to keep my voice from quivering. His books were all over my shelves, his posters on my walls and now, incredibly, he was on the other end of my phone. I paced the room nervously.

"You probably haven't heard of it, it's a small place called Hampton Marsh in the south of New Brunswick."

The line fell silent.

"Hampton Marsh!" he yelled.

"Um, yeah."

"I can't believe it! A country as big as this and you pick Hampton Marsh as your first location! It's a stone's throw from my house, you couldn't have gotten any closer!" The yelling had pushed the phone several inches from my ear. "If you thought I was interested before…I'm really interested now! Say, who are you staying with?"

"Ah, well,…um, we don't really know who we'll be…"

"Well, hurry, get a pen, take this name down."

And so it began. As it turned out this was to be only the first of a series of too-good-to-be-true coincidences that would follow us across the country for the next seven months.

Our plan was to travel across Canada, visiting unprotected wilderness regions that were threatened with destruction from one source or another. Waiting to visit them in a few years' time might prove impossible, as many of them could be irrevocably changed. We wanted to tell their story in words and pictures, as beautifully as we could, to highlight what was good in them and to underscore the environmental challenges facing us all.

Sarah and I were in our early twenties, at an age too old to be considered children, too young to be considered truly contributing members of society. And it was from this standpoint that we wanted to tell our story. In a time of radical change in the world, we found ourselves between the generations. The elderly of today have lived through the most prosperous years of progress in human history. The children of today represent the first human generation to be threatened with the inheritance of an unliveable planet by the end of their lifetime.

Wanting to make our own contribution, we decided to focus on the transition between these two age groups. On the surface enormous changes have already begun in our attitudes and actions. But deeper questions about our values and needs have only barely been scratched in mainstream discussion. Major bridgebuilding work remains to

---

Areas where the water table meets the surface of the earth and is saturated long enough for aquatic-like processes to take place, but are too shallow to be considered a lake or pond are called wetlands. Several different types of wetlands, such as fens, bogs, marshes, mangroves and peat lands, can be found all over the world. Where a wetland develops and what type it is depends on many natural factors such as climate, the physical appearance of the land surface, the mineral or geological make-up of the area and whether or not an area is affected by other water sources such as floodplains or oceans and lakes. Canada has almost one-quarter of the world's wetlands. However, within the last two to three hundred years we have destroyed more than 200 000 square kilometres of them.

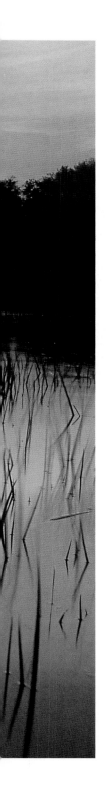

be done. Deciding that any action was better than no action we took out a loan, packed up a van and plunged to the east.

The town of Hampton is surrounded by the Kennebecasis River and Hampton Marsh, the largest wetland complex in New Brunswick. We had heard there was a rather vigorous, locally run campaign to protect the marsh, which was ideal. It seemed to embody the "think globally, act locally" maxim that breaks the enormity of environmental concerns into manageable bite-sized activities that individuals and communities can tackle. Hampton was the perfect starting point for a story about people taking care of their own backyard.

Unfortunately, our timing was not so perfect. We'd been warned before we left that in April most of the marsh would be underwater with the spring freshet, and that it would be quite brown and not looking much like a marsh at all. Never mind, we said. A marsh is a marsh. We'll find something. Besides, we had a schedule to keep!

We should have listened. We arrived to find a brown lake, bordered by houses, that in all but a few locations was too deep to stand in. It was depressing to think about, so we tried not to. Instead we involved ourselves with some of the people concerned with the marsh in the community.

Peter Austin-Smith is a biologist who at the time was the co-ordinator of the Hampton-Kennebecasis Marsh Restoration Project. On our second day in Hampton we toured with him around the area to familiarize ourselves with the situation of the marsh. What we heard was surprising. The issues he described were the sort we would have expected from places like the Amazon basin, not a small town in the south of New Brunswick.

Trees along the edge of the wetland were being removed by landowners for,

The appearance of Hampton Marsh in early April posed some photographic challenges. It was weeks before any foliage emerged.

ironically, a better view of the marsh (deforestation). In the last forty years, 364 new homes have been built on the wetland's shores (overdevelopment). With homes have come people. The village of Hampton has become the town of Hampton and boaters and jet skiers are beginning to clog its waterways (overpopulation). "Nutrient loading," the release of human and other wastes from upstream, is choking the marsh to death (water contamination). Major global concerns all have their counterpart in the microcosm of Hampton. It was an ideal place to start.

Peter was scheduled to lecture about the marsh to a class of grade 12 students at the local high school in a few days' time. He invited us to sit in, as the situation seemed to fit our project perfectly.

A few days later we met Peter in the parking lot and filed into the school, heading for the office. It was a bizarre experience. We'd only left high school a few years ago ourselves. It had been long enough ago to feel totally out of place because of the changed fashions, but not long enough to feel comfortable about heading into the main office. I'd never been very scholastically minded. Formal education ended for me through a slow erosion of missed classes during my final year. What was I doing here?

Coastal wetlands such as Hampton Marsh are often affected by the tides. Every day these marshes are inundated with salt water from the ocean. This temporary flooding raises the water level of the marsh, stirring up nutrients and oxygen. In spring, rain and melting snow further increase the water level of the marsh, completely covering its shoreline for months. It is often not until well into June that the water level begins to drop. This annual occurrence is known as the spring freshet. Trees that normally surround the shores of the marsh show evidence of the height of the freshet by water rings on their trunks long after the waters have receded.

We met the teacher a few minutes later and headed up to the classroom. Sarah and I settled in near the back while Peter organized his overheads and notes. Soon the kids were seated and the lights were blackened. I let myself slump in my chair.

A slide show came first, peppered with dozens of facts and statistics. Everything was covered: nesting box programs, hunting activities, "sustainable" pursuits such as trapping and commercial fishing, and the problem of soil erosion due to the loss of trees and their root systems along the shore. There were plenty of questions along the way, but none so telling as was posed about the saltwater estuary at the southern end of the marsh. A young man raised his arm, cleared his throat and asked, "What can it *do* for us?"

Education about environmental problems is handled very thoroughly in schools today on a cause and effect basis. The kids know about the greenhouse effect and what causes it. They know about overpopulation, our garbage crisis, and why life-guards are wearing sweaters on Australian beaches. But they aren't being taught attitudinal changes. Even the biologist who was teaching the kids was missing the point. To justify diking the marsh and creating ditches and channels all through the area, he used such terms as "enhancement potential" and "control structure." As if somehow we couldn't appreciate and approve of a place like Hampton Marsh until we'd reorganized it, "enhanced" it and "controlled" it.

The single biggest threat to the Earth is the attitude that it must produce for us, or it must resemble some order that we are accustomed to, or it must be "maximized" for some reason or other. With never a thought that the billions of insects, millions of plants, thousands of fish, and hundreds of mammals that make up the living organism of Hampton Marsh have value and deserve respect. Our project title, "Images of Our Inheritance," was not chosen just to express a concern for what will be lost to coming human generations, but to acknowledge a truly common legacy, the future of all life, the inheritance of continued existence.

When we visited Hampton Marsh it was easy to see why so many people care about it, but it was also obvious that some people do not care for it. Between the calls of ospreys and eagles and the slaps of the beaver, angry at our intrusion, we counted

Although wetlands were once seen as wastelands, they have several beneficial functions and are one of the most productive habitats on Earth. Their relatively shallow warm waters efficiently capture the sun's energy to grow tall, lush aquatic plants. Almost ninety different aquatic plant species have been identified in Hampton Marsh, including river bulrush, wild rice, Canada water weed and water lilies.

These plants produce and store food, capture carbon from the air and decaying plant and animal matter, and release oxygen into the atmosphere. By trapping toxins such as heavy metals from pesticides and pollutants from sewage waste up through their root systems, wetland plants act as natural water purification systems, absorbing nutrients and helping recycle them throughout the food web.

The shallow waters and thick foliage provide shelter and food for many different wildlife species. Muskrat are probably the most conspicuous mammal in Hampton's wetland, often seen swimming its waters and slinking around its shores. Some of the wildlife living in wetlands depend on them entirely, or at least partially, for survival. Most Canadian turtles, for example, are unable to live in any other type of ecosystem. Some amphibians, such as frogs, breed and hibernate in wetlands, while certain fish species use wetlands as migration routes to spawning grounds.

In Canada, more than 250 kinds of birds and mammals depend specifically on wetlands for survival and fully one-third of the species listed by COSEWIC (Committee on the Status of Endangered Wildlife in Canada) live in or near wetlands. Migratory birds especially depend on wetlands located along their flyways as breeding, nesting, feeding and resting stations. Black duck, blue-winged teal and the American wigeon are among the most common breeding waterfowl in Hampton Marsh.

Moss-covered rock and trees of the Kennebecasis Valley.

pop bottles half buried in the mud, stumbled over tires and were puzzled by cans of aerosol deodorant rusting in the grass. On the shore hardly thirty paces could be taken without tripping over some garbage. The good news was that they were all things that could be cleaned up easily. The bad news was that people weren't doing nearly enough cleaning.

While the biologist droned on about riparian zones I heard the whispers at the back of the class.

"It's a dump," said one.

"It's full of crap," said another.

Judging by the age and variety of the debris we saw, it's understandable why many kids in Hampton have grown up with that picture of the marsh. In the last half-century Hampton has felt its share of stress from the growing population of the world. And as more people arrive and build, more pressure is put upon the marsh. With every new family, the percentage of careless picnickers and discarded or forgotten belongings rises. There are more disrespectful outdoorspeople and vagrant polluters and waterway accidents — there's even (and I include myself) an increase in the number of bumbling photographers who misplace lens caps. All affect the marsh, and all affect the attitudes of people who come into contact with it. We can't blame young people for their feelings of disregard. The way some of them see it, they haven't got something to care for, they've got something to step around. And who should we blame for that?

In the northeast corner of New Brunswick lies the provincially run Aquarium and Marine Centre. A pamphlet about the facility states it is "Above all…a place to discover an undreamt-of wealth of species which inhabit the Gulf of Saint Lawrence and New Brunswick's lakes and rivers."

We stood mesmerized in front of the largest tanks watching 1.5-metre-long sturgeon circle in blue quietude. There was an incredible variety of fish, and the facility itself was clean, informative and approachable. Every year hundreds of school children pass through its gates to learn about the "undreamt-of wealth of species" that it houses. Beside each tank of fish was a plaque listing six traits about the animals: size, peculiarities, habitat, food, enemies and relation to man. Sarah and I could hardly believe what we read.

Sunset illumines this member of the riparian zone—a border of
vegetation protecting the marsh from the effects of encroachment.

A felled tree serves as an otter's "haul-out" —
a place to consume its catch of clams.

Longnose Gar

Relation to Man: This species is not fished. Bothers fishermen by
getting caught in their nets.

Green Crab

Relation to Man: Of negative indirect importance because it is a serious
danger to shellfish.

Rock Bass

Relation to Man: Of indirect interest since it is eaten by other species
more valued by man.

Atlantic Salmon, juvenile stage, parr

Relation to Man: Of no importance to the fisheries. Highly sensitive to pollution.

Brun Bullhead

Relation to Man: Though of repugnant appearance, its tasty flesh makes it an important recreational and commercial species.

Oysters, Mussels

Relation to Man: Harmful since it destroys a lot of commercially important shellfish.

It went on and on.

We are still teaching youngsters to consider longnose gar a pain in the neck and a nuisance for being killed by our destructive fishing practices. Although oysters make up the diet of endangered animals such as otters, we label them as "harmful." One would think a fish "highly sensitive to pollution" would be extremely valuable as an early warning indicator of contaminated waters, but instead we describe it as "of no importance."

We are teaching that we should respect nature, but only when it's not too much of a bother; that unless we need an animal to make money for us, we can kill it off and consider it unimportant.

From where that grade 12 student was standing, his question, "What can it do for us?" was completely valid. How is he to know any better?

Our next meeting was on the other side of the age divide, with the Hampton Area Environment Group, an assemblage of a half-dozen somewhat past middle-aged men and women. Their meeting had the sort of agenda one might expect: organizing their annual cleanup day, obtaining and repairing litter baskets for the town, discussing avenues for acquiring grant money and setting up donors for their always successful plant sale. Very sensible and effective ideas at a local level. This small group has convinced the Department of Transportation in New Brunswick to change the way they build roads: they lobbied for protective guards to prevent silt from running into Hampton Marsh. A half-dozen people changed a multi-million-dollar activity, and all it took was a few articulate, knowledgeable, organized and committed individuals.

Still, one can't help but consider them the underdogs of the scene. They're up against the deep pockets of the hunters, the city councillors chanting "progress," the often-misguided good intentions of the landowners, the traditional agricultural industry — virtually everyone in the town. Against those odds they are not going to be able to win every single battle. The problem is, their war has no end. When carried to its logical extension, and over the years the defeats are added up, the marsh will inevitably succumb to the pressures. A tree can take only so many swings from an axe, regardless of the time taken between swings. Fighting issue by issue for a place like Hampton Marsh is a losing proposition, unless attitudes change.

Sarah and I happened to be in Hampton for the annual cleanup day. The Environment Group canvassed from door to door, distributed garbage bags, and asked residents to clean the litter out of the gullies and bushes adjacent to their property. Unfortunately it rained that day, so turnout was lower than normal. Sarah and I waded through drainage ditches for about two hours and filled a garbage bag each. It was very rewarding work. Later, whenever we travelled that stretch of road, we found ourselves especially protective of the gullies and grasses we'd cleared of litter.

Despite the best efforts of the local environmental group,
litter spoiled much of the marsh's smaller-scale beauty.

In our minds environmental groups everywhere need two areas of activity: the necessary direct action — cleaning, lobbying and the like — and an effective PR campaign to reach more people with the values of the environmental movement. While Sarah and I were quietly filling our garbage bags along that road, I was trying to figure out how to show people how ridiculous all this garbage was. Why not, I thought, create a mock art exhibition somewhere in the town, displaying the most ludicrous, offensive or unexpected litter collected during the cleanup? Why not highlight the lunacy of what we throw away, and how we live with it, pretending not to see it? There could be a prize — such as a guided tour through the marsh. The point is to make people aware, over and over again, until there is a change in attitude.

Of course, I was a little biased to the garbage exhibit idea myself. I mean, I couldn't lose. How many nine balls from a billiard table do you think anyone else found?

Many people in Hampton see the marsh as a unique habitat that defines their town. Results from a 1993 Hampton Marsh study indicate that more than three-quarters of the population support management efforts in conserving the marsh, but there are conflicting reasons as to why. Some use the marsh for traditional activities such as fishing, hunting and trapping. Others enjoy and appreciate it through non-consumptive activities, the three most popular being canoeing, birdwatching and nature photography. Boaters also use it, especially during the annual spring freshet. Although there is no immediate threat to the delicate nature of Hampton Marsh, the surrounding municipalities are expanding rapidly through urban development. Almost 90 percent of the land bordering the marsh is privately owned and the Quispamsis-Hampton region is one of the fastest-growing in New Brunswick.

Sarah and I attended a meeting organized for "stakeholders" in the marsh. Ranchers, trappers, farmers, hunters and environmentalists were all in attendance. The organizing committee has tried to prove to the various stakeholders that preserving the marsh is good for business, whatever that business may be. Certainly some good has come of it, in terms of curbing negative activities and promoting positive ones. If nothing else, it has provided a forum for opposing camps to express themselves and be heard. However, the problems begin when one tries to define exactly what is and what is not positive or negative. For instance, in late summer the marsh dries out considerably. Ducks Unlimited has bulldozed compounds throughout the marsh to provide more permanent stands of water that encourage waterfowl to linger during the fall migration. Hunters, of course, see this as good. Environmentalists, on the other hand, think that bulldozing and flooding a marsh just so that more birds can be killed is ridiculous.

Setting up a board to deal with the concerns of stakeholders and citizens is a wonderful idea, but its very makeup may be self-defeating. The board has been established to preserve the marsh and at the same time accommodate all the interest groups. Unfortunately, the main concern for the marsh is the amount of pressure being put upon it. Is it possible to keep everyone happy and ensure the long-term survival of the marsh as well? Eventually someone will have to lose, either some of the stakeholders, or some of the marsh.

The interest groups represented at the stakeholder meeting reminded us of how all-pervading environmental concerns are today. Virtually no section of society will remain unchanged or unchallenged by the impending environmental "facelift" of the future. I focused on this point when Sarah and I delivered our own lecture to the same grade 12 class that we'd sat in with two weeks previously.

If nothing else, the human race has proved itself a survivor. It seems that as a species we've always been able to adapt to or overcome any obstacles in our way. The optimistic point of view would suggest that the environmental problems we now face will be no different, but we've never faced a challenge this all-pervasive before. If we are to survive climate change, dwindling water supplies, soil contamination, species extinction, overpopulation and the like, there must be fundamental changes in the way we produce, consume, travel, work and live. Our message to the students was that it makes sense, even at the most selfish level, to know about the threats to the planet. We tried to give everyone in the class a reason for being well informed, even if it was only to save their future jobs and not necessarily to save the planet.

Practical, physical changes are part of the solution. But the lion's share of change will come from the way we see the planet, ourselves, and its billions of other life forms. We need a new way of seeing. A new definition of value. Perhaps even, as author Thomas Berry suggests, "a new sense of what it is to be human."

ALL MY RELATIONS

Cape Breton Island

W e drove until the dirt road whittled down to a dark, thin footpath that we hoped would lead us to our destination.

For thousands of years, the Native American Micmac Nation of the eastern seaboard has considered this its most sacred spot. It was here the god Glooscap had lived in his cave and enacted many of his mythological feats. It was here that he left the world and it was to this place he had promised to return. This mountain and its caves, carved by the pounding Atlantic on the north shore of Cape Breton Island, is the spiritual centre for the entire Micmac Nation.

Dotted along the path, impaled on twigs at eye level, were small, clear plastic bags containing pamphlets from born-again Christians. Their presence underscored the insensitivity of the western world's approach to Native cultures. Sarah and I had decided to include a location of spiritual importance to Native people for our project because their historical relationship with nature is so foreign to the Euro-centric tradition.

We squeezed under fallen trees and clambered over rocks until finally we came to our first magnificent lookout. This had to be it.

We looked out at the red granite dropping sharply sixty metres into the ocean. In the distance lay two islands that, as legend has it, are the remains of Glooscap's broken canoe. Indeed this was a special place. But not only to the eye, as we were about to find out.

"This must be it. This must be," I said as we advanced along the trail. Sarah continued silently in front. "What we need now are some Native people to tell us the story of this place. We need to know something about it."

We hadn't any real contacts for this location. We were miles from anywhere. We didn't know who to call or where to go and our lack of research weighed heavily on me. Not doing much background work on our destinations had been a specific mandate for us. We wanted to let things happen, learn as we went along, with no preconceived ideas. It all sounded good before we left, but now we had no idea of where to go. I tried to convince myself that things would sort themselves out and we continued on, letting the landscape distract us.

An hour later I was balancing myself inside a shallow cave, shielding my equipment from dripping water, when I was startled by a sharp "Hello!" from behind me. I spun around to see three men peering around the rocks, trying to get a look at what I was up to.

"Uh, hi," I said aloud, quickly followed by a silent, "Oh, wonderful." Having people around usually means my work comes to an end. I feel uncomfortable with an audience. But my annoyance quickly turned to anxiety when I remembered I'd left my backpack some distance away.

"Please don't steal it," I thought. "Please don't steal it." I kept nervously glancing in its direction for the few minutes we spent in idle hellos and name exchanging.

The name Mi'kmaq (Micmac) comes from their word *nikmak,* which translates to "my kin friends." The Micmacs lived in wigwams made of spruce and moosewood poles covered with birch bark, often home to as many as fifteen people at one time. A hunter-gatherer society, they killed many types of seafood, from fish and lobster to whales and walruses, and also hunted large land mammals such as moose and caribou. Typical of aboriginal peoples, the Micmac people were respectful of their land and thankful for the animals they killed, always giving something in return for what they had taken. Traditional societies know the life cycles of plants and animals as well as they know their own. Many also name themselves after certain animals or other natural creatures as well as giving names to the wildlife and their surroundings, creating a unique and very personalized connection with the landscape.

Then they got my full attention.

"We've come here for a prayer ceremony," said the oldest of the three, probably in his middle thirties. At first glance I'd only seen his jeans and jean jacket, but now I noticed the band of beads lashed around his neck. His long hair was pulled into a braid at the back of his head and adorned at the bottom with a large eagle feather.

His name was Lonnie, and he was a member of the Micmac Nation. With him were two men in their early twenties, Mike and Kevin. They came here regularly, they said. And once we'd told them the nature of our work they invited us to follow them.

As we filed behind them on the path, I mused on our good fortune. An hour ago I was yearning to talk to Native people about this place, and now Sarah and I were about to take part in a prayer ceremony. It seemed too good to be true. I shook my head, marvelling at the coincidence, as we marched up to a lookout point for a better view.

From there we could see the islands that had once been Glooscap's canoe and another point that hid the cove of the god's dwelling. Farther off were stone pillars in the ocean — women who had been turned to stone by an angry Glooscap. While we

There are at least 800 000 people in Canada who claim to come from a Native background. Belonging to the Algonkian family, one of eight Woodland Indian Tribes, the Micmac are the first known people to settle in Nova Scotia, arriving around 10 500 years ago. Their full territory extends throughout the Maritime Provinces and along the Gaspé Peninsula in eastern Quebec. In the 1500s their traditional way of life was dramatically altered with European settlement of the area.

Glooscap Mountain's old-growth forests were the perfect backdrop to Lonnie's ancient stories and myths.

looked out over this magnificent scene, Lonnie began to share with us the lore that had been handed down among his people for thousands of years. The themes were familiar: living in harmony with nature; respecting all life; deriving not only physical but spiritual sustenance from the natural world. I'd read all this before, I'd seen it all on television, and as he began to talk of his connection with the living world I winced slightly. Here it comes, I thought. This fellow's going to go off on some tangent and I'm going to stand here and get embarrassed and shuffle my feet and wish my mother would yell "Dinner's ready!" from somewhere off in the bush so I could have a reason to run away.

But I was wrong.

Glooscap Mountain, also known as Klooscap or Kelly's Mountain, is located on Cape Breton Island just east of the Cabot Trail, between St. Ann's Bay and the Great Bras d'Or channel. The tip of the mountain at Cape Dauphin and Fairy Hole is covered with old-growth forests and its brilliant red cliffs drop suddenly into the Atlantic. Several caves dot the cliffs facing out towards Bird Island Sanctuary. A narrow trail meanders through the forests, crosses creeks and leads to the caves. It is this part of the mountain that is sacred to the Micmac. And it is this area that has caught the attention of several mining corporations.

Lonnie wasn't muddled or nervous or embarrassed. He was simply communicating what obviously held a lot of importance to him. He was so genuine and articulate that I couldn't help but be convinced of the truth of what he was saying. Totally unlike the clichéd stories I'd seen in books and movies, this was no "this-is-what-it-means-to-be-a-Native-American" speech. He lived these feelings. He was a modern-day person, complete with running shoes and a bandana covering his head, and I had been prejudiced by his appearance. We carried on through the woods, as I mulled over these thoughts.

Mike had come here many times with Lonnie, and they knew the area well. So the first order of business was sharing some of the highlights with us. We climbed down to beaches and crawled into caves, walked up streams and strolled through old-growth forests. All the while we discussed the future of Glooscap Mountain. Mineral interests have been itching to blow up its cliffs for years, but currently there's been a lull in interest. The market has flattened, and the Micmac have put up enough resistance to

Among the mountain's many highlights is its spectacular shoreline, the spot where mining companies want to begin their extractions.

keep would-be developers at bay. However, pressure and the need for these minerals is likely to increase with time, and when the market inevitably makes it a more profitable endeavour, the fight will again be on.

Finally, amid tall straight maples in early spring bud, on the crest of an embankment a short distance from the ocean, we began to search for rocks to build a firepit. Under Lonnie's direction, we left sprinklings of tobacco at any spot where we had taken a rock or piece of wood for the fire. Before tobacco became a major industry, Lonnie told us, it was used by his people for gift-giving and as a token of thanks and debt owed. So we symbolically returned thanks to the Earth with Lonnie's prized tobacco that had been naturally grown free of chemicals or impurities.

Conservation efforts to protect Glooscap Mountain have been hindered partially due to mining proposals. In the early 1990s the market fell out of the aggregate industry on the east coast of Canada. At that time one corporation in particular withdrew its application to mine crushed rock from Glooscap Mountain. Such a large mining project would require an Environmental Assessment (EA) before its approval in order to determine the impact of the project on the environment. EAs are very costly and without the assurance of any economic gain an EA was never conducted.

Although the method of mining to have been used was known, the exact environmental implications of the corporation's mining method were unknown. The project proposed to set off a large dynamite blast daily at dusk. Enough rock would be blasted to keep miners busy for a full day after each detonation. Eventually a tunnel capable of handling docking facilities for large ships would be carved into the side of the mountain just past the Englishtown Ferry. An open-pit mine would lie above this tunnel, presumably hidden from tourist viewpoints along the Cabot Trail.

We arranged thirteen rocks in a circle, but left the east side open, as this was the route that spirits would use to enter our ceremony. One might imagine an air of solemnity would surround the serious business of a prayer ceremony, but Lonnie was far too unpretentious for that. He laughed often and smiled even more. Still, there were serious concerns to address. First he asked us if we had consumed alcohol or narcotics in the last forty-eight hours. None of us had. Impurities in the body would disqualify us from participating in the ceremony. Next, very apologetically, he asked Sarah if she was experiencing her menstruation.

"Don't worry," he said, "it's not a bad thing. A woman is much more powerful at that time, and we would have to be even more respectful of your presence."

He took a braid of sweet grass from his pouch and lit the end so that it burned with a slow ember. A fragrant smoke rose from it and he cupped his hand and wafted the smoke over himself. He started at his feet and brought it slowly up his legs and torso, down his arms and finally in a circle around his head. This was to cleanse the body, and we all went in turn, preparing ourselves in the ancient way.

Lonnie was the first to enact the ritual. He stood on the west side of the firepit, facing the east and silently made a prayer. When he was finished he reached down to the fire and sprinkled tobacco on the flames. He repeated the ritual at the north, east and south, returning to the west for a fifth and final prayer. While the others stared into the fire, we each took our turn moving clockwise around the pit, making our prayers and leaving our offering. We stood motionless and silent, and soon the quiet amplified the humming of the ocean and the whispering leaves around us. It was for them, after all, that we had all come, and in noticing their subtle sounds it seemed for a moment we had received their participation.

Lonnie drew out his prayer pipe. A Micmac artist had carved it beautifully from wood and deer bone and made a gift of it to Lonnie. He filled the end with tobacco

The cliffs of Glooscap Mountain and, in the distance, Bird Islands,
known in Native lore as the remnants of Glooscap's broken canoe.

and lit it, taking three or four long pulls on the mouthpiece to make sure it stayed lit.
He cupped his hand over the bone bowl of the pipe, letting the smoke curl around his
face, and took several long breaths through the wood shaft. Pulling away, he wafted the
smoke around his face, then lifted the pipe above his head with both hands and in an
act of communion said, "All my relations." It was an offering to make peace with all
forms of life.

With a broad smile Lonnie passed the pipe to Mike. We went in turn, always in a
clockwise direction, cleansing ourselves with the smoke, inhaling, offering and cleansing again. We continued until the tobacco, and the jokes about my less than perfect
inhalation, were exhausted.

Next Lonnie removed two decorated rattles from his sack and passed one to Mike. He began a traditional Micmac song and beat the rattle in rhythm. When Mike was ready he joined in, and we watched with the hairs of our necks on end, wishing we could join the celebration.

It was late afternoon by now, and time to go. We disassembled the pit, scattered the ashes of the fire, collected our things and headed back down the trail. Sarah and I, bringing up the rear, saw that occasionally one of the men would step off the path to

---

Long ago, Glooscap, the god of the Micmac people, lived at what today we know as Fairy Hole, on the shore where St. Ann's Bay meets the Atlantic. Glooscap was disliked by an evil wizard who was jealous of the god's great magical powers. One day while Glooscap was away from his wigwam, the wizard kidnapped two young girls and took them down to the shore with the hope of luring Glooscap to him. The two girls shouted for Glooscap while the evil wizard struck them with his spear. He angrily asked them why their great god would not come to their rescue, calling him a liar and a coward. The evil wizard became so outraged he began shouting out as loud as he could for Glooscap to come.

Suddenly the wizard saw Glooscap approaching him along the shoreline. The wizard struck the girls once more and tossed them into Glooscap's canoe. The wizard laughed as he paddled away from shore, shouting back at Glooscap, challenging him to a chase.

In a flash Glooscap magically appeared right beside the evil wizard and before the wizard could react, the two girls had been rescued and were safely back on the shore. Glooscap lifted the wizard and the canoe high up into the air and threw them back down into the deep water. The great power of Glooscap and the ocean broke the canoe in half. Glooscap then broke the gunwales off the canoe and left the broken pieces in the ocean. Today, Glooscap's broken canoe is known as the Bird Islands, a protected sanctuary for many sea birds.

collect the odd pop can or scrap of paper along the way. We arrived back at the cars and exchanged phone numbers and addresses.

"You've been a guide in the true sense today," I said as I shook Lonnie's hand. He smiled his ready smile. They piled into Mike's small hatchback and sped off down the dirt road.

Sarah and I stood staring at each other, half smiling. We knew it would be difficult to communicate the authenticity of what we had seen that day. The teachings and insights that had been shared with us by Lonnie had to come from someone who had that wisdom and understanding in his bones.

But what could we take from it all? Was there not some single bright thought we could carry into our Brave New World like a magic cure? Nothing so simple. We had learned less about Native American traditions than we had about our own. The destruction of wilderness is not simply the cutting of trees or the gutting of mountains. We are nature, and our health and sustenance rely on knowledge of that connection, but we are convinced to see things only in terms of dollars. We are led to believe we are only harming a few insignificant birds or common plants, but we are cutting the legs from beneath ourselves and stealing our own breath.

Suddenly the car reappeared beside us in a swirl of dust and gravel. "We didn't offer you any gifts!" Lonnie yelled from the half-opened window. "I can't believe I don't have anything with me," he said. "My wife and I are right into the crafts, usually my pockets are full of the stuff!" We all laughed.

Then Mike leaned over, "Still, we have these." Dangling from his fingers were a beaded necklace and a leather wrist band.

"Thank you, thank you," said Sarah.

Stones rounded by the Atlantic contrast with Glooscap Mountain's jagged base.

"Hang on!" I said, "Let me find you something!" I rummaged through the shelves of the van. "What have we got? What have we got?" I was frantic. "I can't find anything for you guys . . . . Wait! You're campers, right?" They nodded expectantly. "All right then, I'll give you my most prized camping possession." I fumbled some more, deep in a closet, then spun around, shot out my arm and revealed the prize.

"MY DUCT TAPE!!"

BATTLEGROUND

Temagami

We thought there was plenty of room for him to get through, so we didn't pay much attention to the revving diesel engine behind us. We were deciding where to park on the mud tract leading into the logging cut — police cruisers and television vans already had the best spots on the laneway. Suddenly, a louder rev got our attention. We looked up to see a young logger standing in front of the van sizing us up. He mistakenly identified us as meddlesome protesters and, looking to the truck behind us, shrugged his shoulders.

I turned to see the truck bearing down on us. I threw the van in drive and stomped on the peddle, lurching forward just enough to avoid a collision. It was only as the truck passed that we could fully appreciate its size and what a split-second delay in our reaction might have caused. The wheels alone were taller than our van. If it hadn't scared the hell out of us, we might have seen the Welcome Wagon humour of it. But we didn't. It was a dramatic climax to an already harrowing journey into the Owain Lake forest.

The drive in, along the generously named Rabbit Lake *Road,* nearly killed us, and I'm sure partly killed the van. Potholes, berms and washouts reduced conversation to shrieks of warning and expletives of relief. We were sure she'd never drive the same again.

Although we knew of Temagami and the threat to the old-growth pines in that region, Sarah and I had not planned to make a stop in the northern community. We already had two locations in Ontario and had planned to visit other areas where logging was a concern. We simply couldn't include every wilderness spot in the country that was in trouble; there were just too many of them. However, as activity in Temagami heated during the summer of 1996, news reports travelled the country, protesters set up blockades, police arrested demonstrators, a bridge mysteriously blew up and loggers found spikes in trees. This was the environmental story of the season; we had to make a stop.

We hadn't planned on visiting Temagami, but it became the environmental news story of the year.

Unfortunately there was no one to talk to upon our arrival. Strong winds had brought a small crisis to the nylon shanty town that served as home base for the environmentalists. Most of its twenty or so tents were in need of repair, or in some instances location, and anyone with a shelter sturdy enough to resist the elements was tightly cocooned inside. We parked the van and made tea.

The problems in Temagami were not as black and white as either side would have liked us to believe. Although referred to as "old growth," the area in question, the Owain Lake forest, showed evidence of having been logged at least twice previously. And it was not clear-cutting that was being practised, but a shelter cut, where trees are selectively logged. The majority of the protesters were from Toronto with virtually no local people numbered amongst them. Indeed, most locals resented the environmentalists. The way the media portrayed it, Temagami was practically a treeless wasteland.

Drive about 100 kilometres north on Highway 11 past North Bay, and you'll discover the town of Temagami. Temagami is an Ojibway word meaning "deep water by the shore," a fitting name considering the area has more than 1200 islands in the world's largest network of contiguous canoe and portage routes. Home to many Native people, with artifacts dating as far back as 6000 B.C., Temagami represents a stop on a traditional Native canoe route from Snake Island Lake to Lake Temagami, known as the "birch bark highway."

Today, Temagami is a popular place for wilderness activities and cottage life. The town depends on local tourism for much of its economy. The surrounding wilderness also supports the mining and forestry industries, and has done so for years. The lumber industry began here in the 1920s and has been a way of life for generations of families ever since. The forest industry employs about a quarter of Temagami's population.

Logging affects the entire ecosystem, from the canopy to
the forest floor, where species such as this garter snake live.

When Sarah and I first arrived in town we pulled into a tourist centre and town office hoping to uncover the exact location of the protest. A woman strode past us in the hallway, then burst into a side room.

"Do you know what they're saying about us?" she asked with distress. A woman working at her desk leaned back in her chair to listen. Sarah and I pretended to read a map in the hallway as inconspicuously as we could. "I've just come back from Toronto. Everyone thinks the whole town has been logged. Just look at the news — they make it sound like nothing's left! You know what we've got to do...."

Slam! The door shut their strategizing out of earshot, and we quickly changed our minds about asking questions.

As night fell, Sarah and I ventured to the communal cooking tent to introduce ourselves to the protesters. We met a group of teenagers and twenty-somethings dressed in a style of clothing that was a mixture of the high-tech garments of a Himalayan climber and the brightly coloured knits of the sherpas who guide them. They were busily attending to the menial chores of protester life — hanging clothes and scrubbing dishes. Despite the damp conditions, there was an excitement in camp that night. A young woman had suspended herself high between two trees and tied off to a logging truck below. This is one of the tactics designed to make the practice of logging so unprofitable through lost time that the company eventually packs up and looks for easier pickings. But it was a cold, wet night and news soon came that she had given up her vigil. The damp claimed the spirit of her supporters too, their eyes falling silently back to the cooking fire of the dimly lit tent. Their efforts had not substantially reduced the cutting operation, and every day less was left of the forest.

Nowhere else on our journey would Sarah and I feel the tension of the environmental cause so clearly. The manic mix of reporters, police, loggers and protesters made the forest feel like part carnival, part war zone. The moment we stepped out of the van we were accosted and warned by police. There had been violence here, and threats of violence. The whole forest was uneasy.

We walked through the logging cut, wide-eyed and cautious like hapless army reservists suddenly thrust to the front line. Temagami was a hostile and unnerving place. Our "basic training" of information pamphlets and news articles left us as innocent and falsely secure as any other soldiers. The reality of conflict is ugly and frightening. We didn't want to stay in Temagami long.

Ontario's provincial flower, the trillium,
thrives in the shade of wooded meadows.

Old-growth forests are usually distinguished by very old (at least 120 years), large, healthy trees, standing dead trees, fallen trunks or logs known as nurse logs, and little or no evidence of previous logging. This complex forest structure supports an abundant diversity of plant, animal and bacterial life. In some old-growth forests, red and white pines can grow as tall as ten or twelve storeys.

In Ontario, 99 percent of the old-growth forests are gone. The largest stand of remaining old-growth pine forest in North America can be found in Temagami.

In 1996 protesters fighting to alter the fate of Owain Lake's old-growth pine forest just southeast of Temagami claimed the stand was old-growth red and white pine and home to many unique and rare shrubs and herbs.

Controversy between protesters, loggers and the government grew when the Ministry of Natural Resources claimed the Owain Lake forest was not classified as old growth since they had found evidence of previous tree harvesting before the 1900s and between the late 1930s and early '40s.

There is no question that most logging practices disturb the ecology of a forest, even if only temporarily. However, it is often the equipment rather than the method that causes the most unnecessary harm. Selective cutting still requires roads for massive logging trucks and pathways for skidders. Skidders dragging logs across the forest floor crush all vegetation in their path.

The trucks that transported the felled trees caused the worst damage to the forest. Huge swaths of mud fifteen metres across carved the forest into "blocks," dividing it

By summer's end, spirits were low in the protesters' camp.

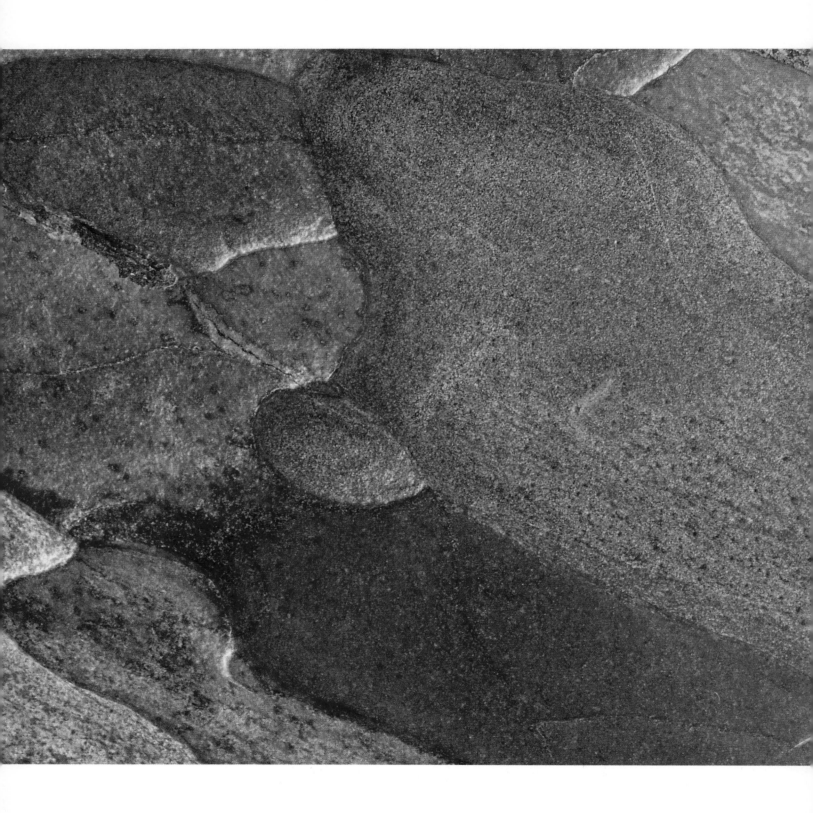

up like some neat suburban neighbourhood. With its mud highways, rushing traffic and busy population of workers, the forest had become a tiny city grafted onto the wilderness.

Our tripod and cameras caught the attention of a passing logger. We guessed his age at somewhere near mid-forty. He was tanned and unshaven with a rounded posture and the thick hands of someone who uses them for a living. At first we thought there might be trouble. But as he approached, the folds of his face creased neatly into a smile and his eyebrows raised disarmingly.

"Are you from TV?" he asked.

After we explained our presence, he told us, in a thick French accent, about a confrontation he'd had with the environmentalists.

"I met up with a group of them," he said. "I tried to tell them why we are here." He shuffled his boots for an even footing in the mud before making his case. "We're only looking to do a day's work. I have a family. I have to feed them. We're not bad people, we're just trying to live like anyone else. I tried to be nice but," he shook his head like some confused father contemplating his teenager, "they wouldn't listen. They pointed fingers and yelled. What can I do?" The protesters seemed as closed-minded to him as he did to them.

Although the environmentalists kept pressure on the logging company all summer, the harvest continued. Each day the trucks passed the protesters' encampment with another load of trees that had taken years to grow and minutes to cut. For the young environmentalists, caught between a vanishing past and diminishing future, the candle burned from both ends. They didn't have time to argue.

Elegant curves and colours give this detail of red pine bark an abstract quality.

More knowledge about the complexity of forest ecosystems has helped change logging practices. In early tree-harvesting days only the strongest, straightest and healthiest pines were cut. But when all the best pines were gone, loggers began clear-cutting, taking all commercially valuable trees. Eventually there were no trees left in some areas, creating a huge threat to the integrity and longevity of the forests and the forest industry. In Temagami clear-cutting is no longer an allowable harvest method.

In the 1996 Owain Lake harvest, loggers used the shelterwood approach, selectively choosing trees to cut. Approximately 30 percent of the Owain Lake Forest block has been harvested using this method. Three cuts in total will take place, each about fifteen to twenty years apart. After the completion of a shelterwood harvest the forest should resemble one where a forest fire has occurred, with standing old trees, dead trees, and rotting trees and branches lying on the forest floor. This selective approach ensures that enough seeds, proper soil conditions and natural forest composition remain so that the forest can regenerate. Sometimes if pine seedlings do not establish naturally, seeds from the felled trees are collected and planted throughout the harvested area. However, if suitable conditions prevail after the harvest, a forest can successfully rebirth itself. Sometimes the level of biodiversity in a recovering forest is actually higher than that of a mature forest and in time a mature woodland will re-establish.

Sarah and I hadn't come to Temagami to find easy answers or choose sides. We came as witnesses, to more than just the facts, to the impulses and feelings — the struggles — taking place in the forest. We had come to learn about it for ourselves, to see it through the eyes of each of its players; we saw the logger as a father, we saw the courage and concern of the protesters.

Nowhere else on our trip did we feel the tensions between industry and environmentalism so clearly.

Our last views were of the forest itself. We walked through the trees, some painted for cutting, some already felled, wondering what the final outcome for the forest would be. We looked at the piles of timber ready to be shipped, the smoking tractors passing by, the standing trees awaiting their fate. We were silent all the while. Listening, or perhaps trying to block out the din of chainsaws around us.

HOME

The Carolinian Zone

Sassafras. Pawpaw. Black gum. Kentucky coffee. No, these are not the ingredients for Louisiana gumbo, but the rare tree species of Ontario's banana belt, the Carolinian Zone. Stretching south of a line extending from the Rouge River Valley in Toronto west to Grand Bend, it is one of Canada's most significant landscapes. It is also where Sarah and I grew up — in the suburbs of Burlington.

Then home was quiet streets, fire hydrants and manicured grass. Neighbourhood dogs. Street signs. There were fences and painted lines and rules. It was a world of order and ownership. All was known. Misshapen cracks on the pale sidewalks seemed the only irregularity.

I was fortunate that my first boyhood home bordered a thin creek. Although surrounded by pavement, a saving ribbon of green stretched for miles in either direction, between homes and parking lots. Its canopy enshrouded a world of mystery. From the outside nothing could be seen. Only by stopping on foot bridges could one glean a peak at the rust-coloured stream of its innards. To a young boy and a street length of friends it was a place of anything and everything. It was a place that called you, then hid you, then slowly poured its life right into you.

Perhaps it was best I moved away before there was a chance for the creek to become small as I grew large. It was never replaced by something grown-up.

Near my next boyhood home was a forest of massive swaying willows and immense fields. Bordered by pavement and more look-alike houses, it too became my real home, walled by wild grass, roofed by boughs.

In a neighbourhood on the other side of town, bordering another creek, was Sarah's house. Meadows and grasses rolled out literally from her back door. Her days were

Most of Canada's Carolinian Zone lies on private property, like this stand of quaking aspen, soon to be developed.

Between 1971 and 1995, Canada's population increased by 7 million, reaching over 29 million people. More than one-third of those people live in Ontario. Sixty percent of the population lives south of a line drawn roughly from Quebec City to Sault Ste. Marie, a small pocket of land that is just over 2 percent of Canada's total land mass.

Hiking its paths almost daily, photographing its naked form. Soon Sarah would join me, field guide in hand, discovering misty sunrises, full moons, and wildflowers by the hundreds. We knew the property as a retreat, as a personal oasis; we had no idea of its significance as a prime tract of the Carolinian Zone. Neither did we know of its half-billion-dollar commercial value.

A few years ago the oil company that owned the property moved. Despite a conservation fight, the land has since been sold to developers. Barring a miracle, it will soon be cookie-cutter houses and video stores. Its coyotes will be gone. Its deer will be gone. Its great horned owls will be gone. So too will its mists and trilliums. Its time has come.

While conservation groups are trying to educate landowners about stewardship programs, the message of preserving a distinct landscape is often drowned out by the considerable financial appeal of development. It's the story of our childhood. Suddenly, the exotic Carolinian Zone had become very personal for Sarah and myself. Those woodlots and fields of our youth, apart from being childhood refuges for us, were

As wild places disappear, so do our chances of experiencing their wonder.

Like these wild mushrooms, the fragmented
Carolinian habitat can be easily overlooked.

probably also islands of a precious and dwindling habitat. We knew we had to include
the Carolinian Zone in our project.

Trying to drum up some locations in the Carolinian Zone, Sarah called one of her
old professors at Waterloo University for advice.

"Oh, there's lots. You could try Backus Woods or Point Pelee or..."

"Right, right, but there's a catch. They need to be unprotected areas."

"Oh...," and a long silence.

Only 2 percent of the Carolinian Zone enjoys a level of protection. But because
of the population density of southern Ontario, the vast majority of the remaining
98 percent is private property, making access almost impossible. Nine phone calls

later we had a shortlist of public areas to explore. Sassafras Woods sounded like a good start.

A study of the woods from twenty years ago could have been written today: "At present the major impact on the area is noise. Traffic from Highway #403 and North Service Road, as well as trail bikes...are major contributors. The trail bikes have also created local soil disturbances and trampled vegetation. This unnecessary destruction of habitat is a continuing problem and may seriously deface the woodlot if it is not curtailed."

Motorcycle tracks were immediately visible in the red clay soil as we began our descent into one of the forest's five valleys. But so were deer tracks and coyote scat. Apart from the Niagara Escarpment to the north, Sassafras Woods is the largest forest in the area, and apparently still capable of supporting large mammals, despite its close proximity to civilization.

The majority of the decline in forest cover within the Carolinian Zone took place 150 to 200 years ago. At least 80 percent of the Carolinian Zone was originally blanketed by woodlands. Today the total forest cover, found mostly in small islands strewn throughout the counties of southwestern Ontario, is about 11 percent. These remaining fragments are so tiny that not even half of 1 percent of them have what are called interior forest.

Interior forests can be found in wood- lands with at least 200 metres of tree cover from edge to edge. They are impor- tant in providing nesting habitat for many bird species, such as the scarlet tanager, sheltering them from predators and the parasitic effects of cowbirds. Roughly 2 percent of the area receives some type of park or public protection. Since the majority of the land in the Carolinian Zone is private, stewardship programs co-ordi- nated through many organizations, such as Carolinian Canada, are made available to landowners in the area.

Carolinian Canada is a program that was created in the 1980s and consists of a mixture of government agencies as well as private and public conservation organizations. The program is the first of its kind in the province to initiate protection of natural habitat through stewardship programs. Landowners receive informative publications and are met personally by representatives of the program. Carolinian Canada also purchases private land that is considered to be threatened, undertakes restoration projects, and initiates education and public awareness. In the future the organization hopes to establish links between protected areas to provide corridors for wildlife to migrate and disperse.

Amazingly, the Carolinian Zone is home to fully one-third of Canada's rare, threatened and endangered species. The checklist reads with poetic allure: swamp rose mallow, Virginia bluebells, oswego tea, flowering dogwood, shagbark hickory, garlon. Whoops — must have crossed notes there. Garlon's actually not a rare Carolinian species, it was the herbicide sprayed in Sassafras Woods. We came upon a mislabelled warning sign stuck in the soil like a gardener's plant label. "Pesticide: Garlon, To Control: Brush." Three hydro lines transect the woods, and apparently the power company needed better access. That seemed to be the motive behind the two dozen felled beech trees down one slope of the valley too. Unfortunately, the integrity of the forest often takes a back seat to the perceived needs of humans.

The Carolinian Zone, which occupies a mere one-quarter of 1 percent of Canada's total land mass, has the bad fortune of being the most densely populated region of the country. Consequently, what is left of Carolinian Canada remains fragmented

A mute swan at sunset in a favourite local creek.

and isolated and susceptible to encroachment. Our next location was a perfect illustration of this.

Iroquois Shoreline Woods, a neat, four-sided municipal woodlot, is bordered by suburban homes, a golf course, a truck plant and a major highway. The same twenty-year-old study that detailed the threats to Sassafras Woods proved ominously accurate in its description of Iroquois. We expected to find two forests of approximately equal size dissected by a main road. But where there had been thickets of red osier dogwood and wild raspberry, and mature stands of red and white oak, basswood and sugar maple on the north side of the road, there was now only a subdivision. The study had warned of proposed development, and argued against it, but apparently without success.

The primary cause of population decline in any species is loss of habitat. Several species, such as the endangered Karner blue butterfly, require unique and often threatened habitat, such as oak savannah, for survival. Forty percent of Canada's endangered wildlife species can be found in the Carolinian Zone, some of which live nowhere else in Canada. Almost one-quarter of the threatened Carolinian species cannot be found anywhere else in the country.

In Canada, tree species such as black walnut, sycamore and the endangered cucumber tree are native only to southwestern Ontario. Other endangered and rare plants found in the Carolinian Zone include green dragon (more commonly known as jack-in-the-pulpit), dwarf hackberry and the small white lady's slipper. Many bird species are also particular to the region, such as the Acadian flycatcher and Carolinian wren. Several migratory bird species—scarlet tanager, least flycatcher and the oven bird, for example—are declining rapidly. Three endangered snake species and the only soft-shelled turtle in Canada are also unique to the Carolinian Zone. Some rare mammal species found in this region include the southern flying squirrel, badger and North America's only marsupial, the opossum.

Conflicts over dwindling resources are only likely to increase in the future.

The day we visited, the forest was veiled in fog, moist and blurred. The vapour cast the forest in a pastel wash. Under such conditions it was easy to feel the Carolinian's exotic character, but just as easy to be confronted by the reality of these woods, as each path we chose led all too quickly to its civilized outskirts. Iroquois Woods is considered the best representation of Carolinian habitat in its area. But it is depressingly small and isolated, making long-term prospects dim. Just how long would it last until urban encroachment took another bite from its side?

The more Sarah and I thought about how best to preserve wild space, the more we realized the need for regular contact with it. Securing remote tracts of land as parks does help protect our natural heritage, but the underlying problem of our disconnection from nature can't be solved with a yearly family vacation.

Wood groves, meadows, wetlands and rivers exist in even the largest cities. They are the "green space," some protected, most not, that pepper our suburbs and countrysides. While they may not have the big-ticket appeal of national parks, they could prove even more vital as instruments of education and barometers of sustainability. The day-to-day experience of nature creates a lifelong relationship with living things — a relationship that often begins in childhood, as was the case for both Sarah and myself.

We have all grown up with areas like these near us. They are the common, overlooked sections of woods and meadows tucked in forgotten corners of our suburbs and cities. Perhaps in childhood there is some unacknowledged awareness of our belonging to these places. Like the untraceable scent of a mother, we know them unconsciously. These parks and woodlots represent a sizeable portion of relatively undisturbed nature that is without protection. We shuffle past them without recognition, but they should be doubly cherished for their close proximity and presence in our everyday life. These areas could be schooling us in our changing role on this planet. They could be our re-introduction to enchantment.

WATER

Lake Ontario

We skidded to a stop, grabbed our gear and sprinted madly for the shore. I crouched low, hiding from the thunder above me, wrestling the camera onto the tripod. Sarah opened the umbrella, shading the equipment. I'd waited five years for this moment. Five years for a storm like this, for the lightning to be bright enough and consistent enough and over the right portion of the lake, at just the right distance, with the last wanings of dusk still lighting the clouds. It was perfect. There was just enough light to level the horizon through the viewfinder. I was shaking with excitement. The shutter clicked. Bang! A bolt struck smack in the centre. I grabbed Sarah and kissed her as thunder rolled above us like applause. We'd done it. At last. It was perfect. Absolutely perfect.

We spent two hours there on the shore of Lake Ontario, watching the storm drift across the border. Long enough to eventually be dried out by the warm summer wind that filled the vacuum behind the front. The last flicks of light fell like tiny bombs on the horizon. We sat and watched, exhausted and content.

Of course, at that moment we didn't yet know how badly I'd screwed up. It was dark looking through that viewfinder. And in the rush to capture the lightning I'd forgotten a crucial detail, a detail I'd never forgotten before. I looked over the images — frame after frame of beautifully composed, perfectly exposed, magnificently lit, blurry images of lightning. In my haste I'd forgotten to focus the lens to infinity. Five years of waiting. Dozens of other attempts. Ruined by a fractional turn of the focus ring. It was a career low.

It could have been worse. In fact, it had been worse at our previous locale. Originally Sarah and I had chosen a location further down the Great Lakes system, Lac St. Pierre in the St. Lawrence.

Lac St. Pierre is well known for its large breeding colonies of birds. But it is becoming equally well known for the industrial pollution damaging the aquatic and

Storm waves batter the shore of Lake Ontario.

terrestrial life of the region. Sarah and I saw an opportunity to get great pictures of large numbers of birds and to discuss the problems of industrial and agricultural pollution. We bought ourselves a Zodiac and a used two-stroke engine and headed for the town of Sorel.

From the start we knew we were in trouble. We'd arrived too late; most of the birds had disappeared. A tour with a sightseeing outfitter only helped confirm the dark prospects. There weren't many birds left and the few colonies that were still populated were off-limits. We'd come a long way and invested a lot in being here; we couldn't go home without giving it our best shot. So we assembled the Zodiac and set out on the water determined to find something to photograph.

After a few hours of exploring the islands and inlets of the lake, just as we were beginning to think there might be a reason to stay, the engine almost died. We couldn't go more than quarter-throttle without it threatening to blow up. We were many kilometres away from the van and the sun was quickly going down. Soon it was pitch dark. We hobbled along, with no light to see by or advertise our presence.

Slowly a faint hum began to sound over the banging of the motor. It grew louder. And louder. Sarah turned to look behind us. "Jaaames," she said, staring wide-eyed. I turned to see what looked like the entire skyline of the lakeshore moving toward us. It took a few moments for my brain to realize the hundreds of points of light were not homes on a distant shore, but actually the lighted windows of a huge ship. Minutes earlier we'd have been flotsam. As it was, we narrowly escaped with all our parts intact, and a more certain decision to pack up and go home.

To cap things off, we got a flat tire on our way out of the region, as if to punctuate our departure with the admonition, "And stay out!" Two days later the devastating floods of the Saguenay region began.

We shifted the location upstream, so to speak, to Lake Ontario. The waterways of the Great Lakes are all interconnected, so in a way we could tell the same story from a different location. The idea got us thinking about the way water moves from place to place — sometimes through aquifers, sometimes through weather patterns, and sometimes through a six-cylinder van that loads up and disperses water from its reservoir as its occupants need it, like a four-wheeled cloud motoring the freeway.

Water is always on the move. We look out over a body of water like Lake Ontario and think it separate, isolated, from our own bodies. But the water within us is moving too. Soon it will leave our bodies as well and be replaced by water from somewhere

Misty sunrise, Lake Ontario.

else. And it too will move, again and again, like a stream running from person to person to river to cloud to plant to lake to person. Over and over, one continuous exchange of water, of which we are but one temporary holding tank.

Threats to our water supply aren't restricted to certain environments. Water isn't an endangered place. It's an endangered substance that happens to be a prerequisite for life. In freshwater form, it is comparatively rare. A mere 3 percent of the world's water supply is fresh; the rest is salt water. Of that 3 percent, two-thirds is locked in ice at the polar extremes of the planet. The remaining 1 percent of fresh water is only

---

Although much improved since the 1970s, the quality of water in the Great Lakes is far from good. Many of the chemicals found in the lake today were actually dumped by industrial factories about half a century ago.

One of the problems with attempts at cleaning up the Great Lakes or any body of water is that many chemicals may never be successfully removed or broken down. Creating even greater headaches for scientists, toxic substances can enter into a waterway following several different paths, making it hard to pinpoint the source of the pollution. For example, while some toxins are directly released into the lake through industry and effluent pipes from sewage treatment plants, other substances, such as pesticides from farmland and airborne particles, may travel some distance, even thousands of kilometres, before entering a body of water. The more indirect the source and entry of the pollution, the more difficult it is to enforce regulations.

Old, abandoned chemical dump sites can also cause problems. Along the American shoreline of the Niagara River are over 60 chemical dumps. These dumps are *all* abandoned and they are *all* leaking. Every day over 300 kilograms of contaminants are spilled from these sites into the Niagara River, slowly riding the current into Lake Ontario.

Pollutants biomagnify as they ascend the food chain.

50 percent available to us, as the other 50 percent is too far below the earth's surface to extract economically. So on this "big blue planet" we can be nourished with only .5 of 1 percent of the world's water supply — a water supply that is becoming increasingly polluted and increasingly depended on by an ever larger world population.

Choosing the Great Lakes for a discussion on fresh water might have seemed an obvious choice, but the idea struck Sarah and I as quite novel. We had grown up on the shore of Lake Ontario. It had been the backdrop to our lives, a place so close, so common that we never really considered it much.

There aren't many "secret places" left on the shores of Lake Ontario. Parks, private property and industry form a continuous ring around this massive body of water.

Canada holds 9 percent of the world's freshwater supply. The majority of this fresh water is found in the Great Lakes, the largest freshwater system in the world.

Early settlers were drawn to this region because of its milder climate, ease of transportation, and industrial power and agricultural possibilities. This is common throughout the world. One-third of the world population lives within 10 kilometres of a lake or ocean. Today more than 33 million people live in the Great Lakes region.

Luckily, as a boy I found a secret beach that to this day remains unowned — a place I soon shared with Sarah.

The spot has blessed me several times. It was here I'd taken one of my favourite images, a winter scene of ice-covered branches at sunrise. It was here that I found a canoe, washed ashore after a storm one bleak spring morning. From that cove Sarah and I have watched parades of geese and swans stretch and waken, swarms of buffle-heads navigate burning sunrises and drizzled mornings that blend sky, horizon and water into one seamless shimmering screen of grey.

It was also the place we flushed our toilet into.

Perhaps not directly, but somewhere not far away an unlabelled pipe excreted the city's waste to the same effect. The lake was also where we got our water, to clean with, bathe ourselves and drink. And even with all the time we spent on that secret beach, we never gave it much thought. Turn a tap, drink. Pull a chain, flush. We never bothered with the connections between those actions and the lake we visited.

Toxins in the Great Lakes are causing deformities and infertility among many species of wildlife.

Nutrients and stored energy pass through individual species as they eat and are eaten by other species in the food chain. Humans are at the top of all food chains. The interconnections of food chains form food webs. All members of the food web are adversely affected by toxic substances in their environment.

While some pollutants may be relatively minute in open water, their concentrations can increase by millions of times as they work their way up the food chain, a process called biomagnification. For example, humans are at greater risk of exposing themselves to toxins by eating one fish from a polluted lake than by drinking the water the fish came from.

Scientists are concerned about the long-term effects of low-level exposure on the human immune system. Some fish and wildlife species in and around contaminated water habitats have developed severe physical deformities, such as crossed bills and tumours, as well as sustaining damage to their reproductive systems.

Living in a van did get us thinking about water. We travelled with a 20-litre collapsible plastic water holder that seemed always on the verge of depletion. We had to conserve every drop, whether carefully splashing our dishes or dripping water on our toothbrushes. We didn't want to waste any of it, since finding places to refill often proved awkward and inconvenient. But, by virtue of such strict rationing, we quickly became aware of how carefree and wasteful we'd been with water in everyday life. "When the well's dry, we know the worth of water."

Sarah had certainly learned the worth of keeping aquatic habitats intact. Cootes Paradise in the far western corner of Lake Ontario is well known as the site of one

Bitter cold brings ice and fog to the surface of Lake Ontario.

of the largest restoration projects in North America. She volunteered four weekends to assist Project Paradise with the Bay Area Restoration Project.

With a group of other volunteers, Sarah planted marsh vegetation to replace what had been lost in recent years largely because of the introduction of carp. The non-native species stirs up sediment and uproots aquatic plants while feeding and spawning in shallow waters. A highly successful fishway, a bridgelike barrier between shores prevents carp from entering the marsh from the lake, but allows the movement of native species. The fishway and replanting, among other projects, are rebuilding the ecosystem.

Clad in chest waders, the volunteers were warned by a researcher not to even *touch* their faces, as the area was laden with extremely high *E. coli* levels. "Turn a tap, drink. Pull a chain, flush." Suddenly this did mean something to Sarah.

Our experiences helped Sarah and I see water differently. Lakes and rivers were no longer removed and isolated from us. We began to see ourselves as part of the water cycle; we began to see the lake as part of us.

THE UNCOVERING

The Great Sandhills

"**D**on't worry, there'll be one here for sure."

Saskatchewan's Highway 32 is a lonely stretch of road.

"Damn."

With very few gas stations.

The town of Lancer was a strikeout. Ditto for Portreeve. Lemsford had a gas station at one time but it was now closed. We drove past, our eyes tracking each rusted pump, like the proverbial skeleton in the desert.

"Never mind, there's lots of gas left," I said, as another ping of vapour echoed from the tank. Just getting to Sceptre, our destination, seemed like the climax of the story. We made it, and there was a gas station in town, too.

Amazingly, Sceptre also had a small museum. I suspect not many visitors stopped there; we waited half an hour in the van before an elderly man appeared from across the highway to let us in. I recalled how Freeman Patterson had let us know we could call him if we found ourselves feeling alone somewhere in "phone-booth Saskatchewan." This must have been where he meant.

Inside the museum we got our first impressions of the sandhills we'd come to document. Surrounding the town was flat prairie and it was hard to imagine the presence of enormous sand dunes just a few short kilometres away. They were unlike anything else we would see on our journey and after looking at the exhibits we were eager for first-hand experience.

From the back of town a sand road led to the dunes. On our first day, back in Hampton, we buried two wheels in the ditch while busily looking at the marsh. We didn't want to repeat the experience out here in the sand, as could easily happen. The

Coyote and beetle tracks transect the wind-sculpted pattern of the sands.

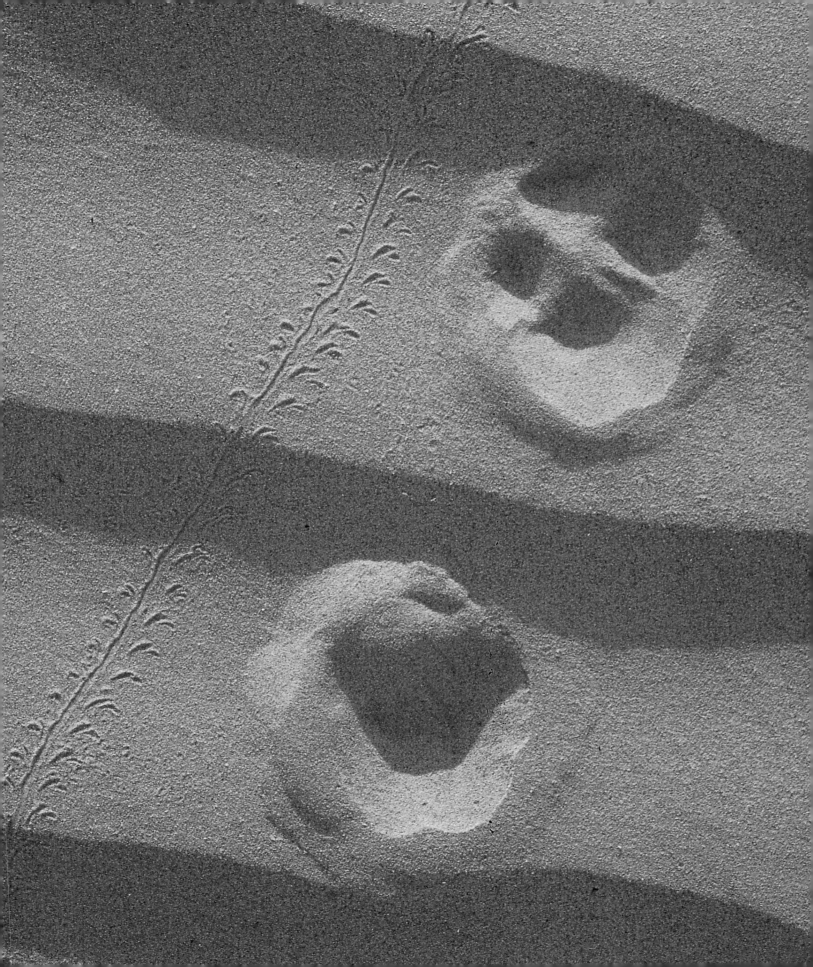

We encountered many of the Sandhills' inhabitants —
mule deer, coyotes, raptors — but no rattlesnakes.

road was narrow and nerve-wracking, especially for our Zeppelin of a van, but not without interest. We soon came to cowboy-boot curve, a posting of twenty or so presumably lost cowboy boots, touted as "The Head of the Hills Inn." Next was a Saskatchewan traffic jam — a herd of cows taking a siesta in the middle of the road.

Ecologically, cows hardly qualify as suitable inhabitants of the delicate Sandhills habitat. Strangely, though, their stolid presence seemed more fitting than the skittish mule deer of the same parts. Occasionally, a baritone "moo" would escape over the undulating curves of the landscape, advertising the presence of the bovines, but not their exact location. The cows inch slowly along, the perfect counterpart to the dunes, as though the winds were pushing them along as well. They are as odd and surprising to see in this landscape as the landscape is to see at all. Noticing a cow or distant dune has a domino effect. Spot one and dozens more appear in succession all around you.

The Sandhills can be a raw place in the oppressive heat of July. Virtually treeless, hardly a spot of shade can be found to escape the sweltering press of the day. The vegetation of the region is scrubby and dry, clinging precariously to life on a foundation of sand. Scattered about, active dunes devoid of any flora create a landscape that is a study of starkness and subtlety. Pushed by the western wind, the moving dunes can swallow whole trees in their path, or expose scoured bones in their wake. Conversely,

---

Tucked away, south of the South Saskatchewan River and north of the Trans-Canada Highway, lies a remarkable desertlike region called the Great Sandhills. Almost 2000 square kilometres, this area represents the Canadian Prairie's largest connecting dune system and the most extensive cluster of active and stabilized dunes in colonized regions of Canada. Although active dunes account for only a very small portion of the total area, they represent dunes with the greatest relief. Most dunes in the Great Sandhills don't reach 15 metres in height and only a few surpass that.

Just over 300 square kilometres of the Sandhills is privately owned. The remaining crown land is leased out to private mineral interests or grazing co-operatives. Agriculture, primarily cattle grazing, is the most dominant use of the land in the Sandhills. Other uses include utility, oil and gas transmission lines, the development and exploration of petroleum, and recreational activities such as hunting and bird watching.

Only one road, located in the southern and less sensitive portion, crosses the Sandhills. One other road located in the northwestern portion provides access to the active dune systems. Neither of the two roads is part of the regular road network and they see only the bare minimum in maintenance.

Deserts are areas where evaporation exceeds the amount of rainfall to varying degrees. Some deserts are extremely hot and dry, creating a harsh environment for life to evolve. The Sandhills, however, has a diverse enough landscape and receives sufficient moisture to sustain a variety of plant and animal species.

The main types of vegetation are shrubs, grasses and forbs, some of which are rare, such as yucca and prickly milkvetch. These low-lying plants are specially adapted to grow in areas with little rain and dry sandy soils. The secret lies with the structure of the plant. Some have extensive root systems that spread out, covering as much surface area as possible in order to gather moisture, while others grow long roots that extend deep into the sand to find moisture. Other plants have developed special leaf functions, often with a waxy coating to help retain water. Although few and far between, the Sandhills is home to two tree species more common to areas of moist soils, trembling aspen and plains cottonwood.

The vegetation supports a variety of grazing mammals, such as white-tailed deer, mule deer and pronghorn antelope. Other common fauna include coyote, red fox and Hungarian partridge. Also making their home in this semi-desert are several threatened and endangered species, including the burrowing owl, ferruginous hawk and loggerhead shrike. A study focusing on flora and fauna of the Sandhills found no reptiles in the area.

the dunes can be cut in two by the tracks of a single beetle, or be overcome by simple grass, a blade at a time.

An atmosphere of quiet tension pervades the dunes. It is a place where you have to shake your head to refocus your eyes. It is not pretty or sad, and doesn't elicit any

With little shade, temperatures soar under the open sky of the prairie.

Cattle grazing and oil and gas development are essential components of Saskatchewan's provincial and local economies. The Great Sandhills contains one main community pasture consisting of a co-op of ranchers and grazing leases. More than 130 000 hectares of grazing land are under lease. The native grass species that grow here support sixty different cattle-grazing operations.

In the past, grazing capacities were determined using a cow and calf of standard weight. Due to modern farming technologies cows are up to 30 percent larger and this size increase, demanding larger appetites, now threatens the carrying capacity of the native grass species.

Tourism is also an important economic activity for the province and the local residents and rural municipalities would like to preserve the Sandhills as a day-use park to help promote awareness and educate the public about the functions and values of its unique arid habitat.

immediate thought. A quiet persistent wind washes the land constantly and the dunes seem to hum. If ever there was a place to stop and be taught by the silences of nature, this is it. Its balance of delicacy and toughness heightens the senses to new levels of perception.

Our first ventures onto the landscape were quite comical. The minute we set foot on the coarse grass of the prairie our primal fear of snakes took over. We were convinced at any moment we'd encounter a rattlesnake.

Our initial tactic to avoid this was the cautious approach. Every step involved a meticulous mine-sweep, studying the ground for movement. Our eyes zipped back and forth in front of us until finally we'd come up for air and find our bearings.

Thunderclouds gather over the Sandhills.

Next we tried the quick march. Eyes up, backs straight, we double-timed our advance to the next dune with the rigid endurance of a palace guard and the utter impatience of a hot coal walker. The latter technique worked best for me. Not only could I see where I was going, but the pace was a good match for the incessant, high-pitched mosquitoes invading my ears. Sarah took things a step further, combining both the mine-sweep and the quick march, advancing at a near run with protective rubber boots on her feet while thrashing the grass with a long stick. It amazes us still that anyone would actually stop and talk with two people acting this way, but they did.

We met a university professor, hiking the hills with his wife. Sarah laughed later about how much he looked the part—a Tilley hat tied too tight around his chin, a slight paunch taxing the waist of his walking shorts, and sandals with socks as thick as his beard and about the same colour.

"If predictions are right," he said, gazing across the dunes, "this will extend halfway down the States pretty soon. Global warming," he added, to which we nodded in resigned agreement.

In early 1991, the Saskatchewan government established a planning committee to develop a land-use plan for the Great Sandhills. At the same time a temporary moratorium was put on any new development, such as oil and gas exploration, in sensitive areas of the Sandhills. The plan focuses mainly on the moratorium area with the goal of maintaining the landscape of the Sandhills for economic, cultural and social purposes. Areas were divided into zones ranging from prime protection to multiple use, in order to help determine the type of management required. Objectives of the plan include maintaining biodiversity, protecting unique landscapes and heritage resources, ensuring sustainable use of renewable resources and ensuring environmentally sound management of non-renewable resources.

Moon above dunes at sunrise.

Scientists predict that countries in northern latitudes, such as Canada, will undergo more extreme changes in temperature due to global warming than other areas. In the next hundred years, the Earth's temperature may climb by two degrees Celsius. Sea levels could rise 15 to 95 centimetres. The increased temperature would allow the air to retain more moisture, creating long periods of drought punctuated by extreme rainfalls. It was a frightening thought. Until then we'd seen the Sandhills as a rare and beautiful landscape. But with those two words, "global warming," it transformed into a cancer, threatening the breadbaskets of North America. All the words we might have used to describe it before were now replaced by just one. Dustbowl.

By 1991 a land use strategy was passed and the provincial government agreed not to sell any leases to gas and oil companies for the following three years. That period is now over and gas and oil companies are free to purchase mineral rights within the Sandhills. However, according to a 1994 municipal bylaw, no new development can occur in the Environmentally Sensitive (ES) Zone, one of the three zones which covers most of the Sandhills region, without a permit granted by the municipalities. For example, a petroleum company could potentially purchase land in the ES Zone, yet would be unable to develop or explore it without first obtaining approval, which is highly unlikely, from the local municipality. In addition to the bylaw, three "prime protection areas" have been established in the Sandhills for the purpose of setting aside intact natural habitat. The mineral rights to these areas have since been bought back by the Saskatchewan government.

It was ironic. Sarah and I had come to the Great Sandhills to document a "threatened" environment, but now the environment itself represented a threat. Where we once envisioned park boundaries to protect it, we now imagined barriers to contain it. If global warming did continue, the droughted land might spread from these very hills, bringing the calamity of the 1930s with it. Suddenly we had to rethink our reasons for being there.

A night on the hills helped put things in perspective. We hiked out with our gear in late afternoon and set up camp on the sand. The moon rose, the mosquitoes left and soon the cool wrap of twilight fell. We sat on the dunes and watched each star burn its

Though beautiful, the Sandhills confronted us with the possibility of global warming.

way through the coming night, as if called into presence by the distant yips of coyotes around us. With judgements gone, predictions gone, worry gone, we could sit and absorb the landscape we were a part of. As thoughts, cares, judgements fell away, we returned to that place of our childhoods — a simple wonder and pleasure in the beauty around us.

POSTCARDS
&FRAGMENTS

Banff National Park

While primarily we were intent on visiting unprotected areas of the country, we thought a stop at Canada's first national park was also in order. Although protected, Banff is undergoing its own crisis. Many conservationists worry that the integrity of the park is being undermined by Banff townsite, a fully functional community existing within park boundaries. This special relationship between humans and nature has forced the consideration of an unsettling possibility: that park status may not ultimately protect wild spaces. Reconciling human habitation with wilderness preservation may mean that we cannot separate areas such as Banff park from Banff townsite; a more integrated relationship may be necessary. This larger challenge attracted us, so, on a whim, while sitting in the desert, we decided to pack up and go. Creature comforts are few and far between when you live in a van on back roads. This was to be our treat. We were going to Banff.

Originally established in 1885 under the name Rocky Mountain Park, Banff was the first national park in Canada and the third in North America. Created as a 26-square-kilometre reserve set aside to protect the mineral hot springs on Sulphur Mountain from settlement and private development, Banff now boasts a total area of 6800 square kilometres.

Named after the town of Banff in eastern Scotland's county of Banffshire, Banff is derived from the word *bunhaimb,* Gaelic for "mouth of the river." Today

Banff National Park is a UNESCO World Heritage Site and is part of four connecting national parks, three provincial parks and several wilderness areas. The original Rocky Mountain Park Act emphasized the use of the park as a place of pleasure, for the enjoyment and benefit of all Canadians. In 1930 the National Park Act stated that the park remain "unimpaired" for future generations. Today Parks Canada faces an intricate, complex mandate that places ecological integrity above international tourism.

Lichen-covered rock.

We pulled into town, showered up, then hit the promenade. Dinner first, then shopping. Sarah and I were trying to buy all our Christmas gifts as we travelled the country. Between morning and evening shoots, we prowled Banff's main drag in search of bargains.

Still, we couldn't help but feel a little guilty. We had come to Banff with the intent of exploring serious environmental concerns, of turning a grim eye to the development and exploitation of the park. And here we were, eager participants swept up in the bustle and buying of Banff. The guilt hit home while we were sitting on a park bench, on a huge patio, in glorious sun, ice cream cones in hand, watching tourists photograph Lake Louise. We were grinning from ear to ear. But should we have been?

Fifty years ago the population of the town of Banff was close to 2400, with just under 460 000 tourists visiting the park each year. At that time there was limited overnight accommodation, hence the park was mainly used for day activities such as fishing, hunting, hiking and horseback riding during summer months, and skiing during the winter season.

Since the 1950s Banff has grown considerably. In 1995 the combined resident population of the town of Banff and Lake Louise was at least 9000, the largest community within a national park in North America. This same year Banff received 5 million tourists, more than any other Canadian park. On top of the growing residential population and visiting tourists, an additional 3 million individuals travel through the park via the Trans-Canada Highway every year.

Today, Banff is a bustling year-round destination with several commercial ski hills and cross-country trails, a 27-hole golf course, 2500 car-based serviced campsites within 14 different campgrounds, about 1500 kilometres in trails, a commercial downtown core with well over 100 restaurants and half as many hotels, a divided four-lane highway and a rail corridor. The tourist industry of Banff National Park is the driving force behind the local and provincial economy. In 1995 alone, visitors spent more than 700 million dollars in the park. Some studies suggest that if future trends are consistent with those of the last five decades and no new regulations are enforced, the annual number of visitors could potentially reach 19 million by the year 2020.

high heels we had just passed, or us, garbed with enough belts, buckles, straps and Gore-Tex to walk on the moon's surface? Frankly, we were all dressed inappropriately for that trail; any five-year-old in play clothes would have been better suited. The point was, though, that we all wanted to experience ourselves as a part of it, and that

Wildflowers bloom in profusion throughout the park's valleys.

Combine the recent urban expansion in the town of Banff and hamlet of Lake Louise with a decrease in funding from Parks Canada and an increase in park visitors, and the resulting mixture can go very sour. Banff's natural habitat and its wildlife are the areas most affected. The Trans-Canada Highway and other nearby roadways fragment the ecosystem, creating barriers for migrating animals. In 1995 only four male grizzlies were known to have regularly crossed the Trans-Canada Highway and no females had crossed highways or used wildlife under- or overpasses. Railway and highway collisions are the leading cause of death for many wildlife species.

Development around the towns of Canmore, Banff and Lake Louise reduce natural habitat for large predators such as grizzlies. Wandering grizzlies and other large mammals viewed as dangerous are often destroyed or removed from parks, towns and campgrounds in the interest of public safety.

The park's aquatic habitats have also suffered. More than 40 percent of the water systems in the Banff–Bow Valley have been regulated for human use. Funding difficulties and a privatized management system have affected the forests. Suppressing natural wildfires inhibits the natural life cycle of forests; aging vegetation can increase the possibility of future uncontrollable wildfires and change the natural forest composition.

would naturally reflect who we were as individuals. There can be no hard-and-fast rules of how to relate to nature.

It is ironic that as we rush to protect more and more chunks of wilderness and include them in our park system, we are perpetuating the separateness that is at the root of environmental problems. By labelling areas as parks, as "special," we are drawing boundaries around the natural world and segregating it. By denouncing human presence and impact on natural areas we are excluding ourselves from nature. While

Banff has always been the model for our changing relationship with nature.

the intentions behind this may be good, the result is not. A small park system — even a large park system — cannot survive if, on the rest of the planet, we pour toxins into the sky and over the soil.

Because of its overdevelopment Banff is currently judged harshly as a park, but that is a result of our misidentification of it. Banff has metamorphosed, or rather, is metamorphosing. At its founding Banff was a small townsite surrounded by nature. It then expanded into a large park threatened by development. Today it is fusing town and park together. The mistake has been considering it as unique. It should not be a model of a different, special park system, but a model for all our living areas in all regions of the country.

The challenge is not to convince people of how wonderful places such as Banff are, but of how beautiful and magnificent our own backyards are. Banff is no longer a model park, and that's a good thing. It is a model habitat, a testing ground where the overriding concern is the health of the ecosystem. Removing people from a habitat does not mean long-term survival of that habitat. Segregating ourselves from pristine areas, and not monitoring activities outside those areas, will only slowly infect the borders of any place we cordon off.

Wherever people go they will alter the landscape around them. Like all settlements, Banff has changed and developed. But unlike them, development is policed by a concern for the health of the environment. People must live, travel and conduct business, but all are weighed against the impact on nature.

The large environmental organizations around the globe set the agenda for environmental reforms because of their power to reach people. But what if their agenda is fundamentally flawed? They often use blanket statements such as "take only pictures,

Morning shadows on Peyto Lake.

The Tombstone Mountain region represents a large expanse of wild habitat for many different species, a home and way of life to people of the First Nations, as well as potential grounds for mining exploration and extraction. Recommendations to protect the Tombstones and its surroundings began in the mid-1970s.

The first proposal for a Tombstone Territorial Park was suggested by the Tr'on dek Hwech'in First Nation. The original 100 000-hectare boundary included vital land surrounding the Tombstones, including the Blackstone Uplands to the north of the Tombstones. This is the minimum size capable of supporting populations of large mammals such as grizzly and black bear, woodland and barren-ground caribou, Dall sheep and moose. It would also support numerous arctic bird species surviving at the southern limit of their range as well as rare plant communities. The proposed boundary included nine distinct ecosystems.

In the early 1990s the territorial government altered the original park proposal by drastically reducing the size to 38 700 hectares, thus eliminating seven of the nine ecosystems. This meant that many of the biologically rich regions north of the Tombstone Mountain Range would receive no protection.

other, sharing stories, but by night's end only a few remained. A young man across the fire was talking about where he had travelled in the last few days, and the man he had travelled with, Patrick Morrow.

"Pat Morrow!" I exclaimed, interrupting him. "You were with Patrick Morrow, the photographer?"

"Yes," he said. "Didn't you see him? He was here tonight, sitting there, right next to you."

We were unprepared for the grandeur of the Tombstones;
they were unlike any other part of the country.

of the day to kill before we left and were invited by Pat and Baiba to go shooting some stock from a lookout above Dawson. On our way up the hillside we came upon a stand of brilliant yellow aspen framed by a flawless blue sky. The van came to a stop and we all piled out to get some pictures.

I had been rather starstruck by Pat and Baiba since we met them, but now was my chance. I wasn't about to be outdone. I was going to appear as professional as them. I squinted my eyes and measured the scene, then paced thoughtfully about deciding on the best angle. Squat down? Up high? Rub my chin. Aha! Slickly I fastened the tripod head, looked away and clicked the shutter release. Very smooth. Very calculated. I didn't allow myself to get too excited by the scene, that would be uncool. Anyway, I'd done this a thousand times before, right? I was an old pro. So I whisked my camera away and sauntered back to the van. Very smooth. Very calculated.

It wasn't until we started down the road again that I realized I had been playing James Bond, the photographer, with no film in my camera. In all that time I hadn't taken a single frame. Very smooth.

That evening we had dinner with a friend of Pat and Baiba in Dawson. Partway through our spaghetti and caribou sausage meal I choked back a laugh. In response to the questioning looks, I explained that Yuri Peepre had told Sarah and me earlier in the week that northerners hated it when maps of Canada only showed the southern provinces and not the northern territories, as though the north is not important enough to be included in maps of the country. Then I pointed to the enormous map of the Yukon occupying the entire wall behind us. "Seems like you're overcompen-sating a bit."

Pat and Baiba guided us through the Tombstones' remote mountain passes.

Our hostess laughed. "Yes, and come to think of it, about every house up here has a map just like it. I'd never thought of it like that before."

The real reason she had the map was because she spent a lot of time travelling across her home territory. She proceeded to point out all the places she'd been, and all the places she planned to go. Exploration is still a daily theme in Yukon life. In fact, Sarah and I wound up borrowing some camping gear from our hostess.

After a two-day weather delay we found ourselves crouched above our packs, our faces turned from the dust and stones pelting us from the helicopter's prop wash. We were away.

Helicopters are not safe. At least, they don't feel safe. Imagine five people crammed into a Volkswagen beetle, suspended by wind a kilometre in the air and being shaken violently, and you have a taste of a helicopter ride through the mountains. But more shocking than the ride was the temperature when the helicopter landed. The difference in climate a few short mountain ridges apart was remarkable. We kept the blood moving by setting up our tents, but not before busily photographing stark Tombstone

---

The Canadian Parks and Wilderness Society, the Tr'on dek Hwech'in Nation and other conservation organizations have now developed a new park proposal. It not only includes the original core park area of 100 000 hectares but at least 25 000 to 50 000 additional hectares. Within the revised park boundary lie three more distinct regions designated as zones needing special management.

Not only would the larger Tombstone Park benefit the wild northern habitat, wildlife and Native cultures, it would also benefit Yukon's tourism industry and the local economy by preserving one of Canada's most remarkable wilderness landscapes.

Light in the distance illuminates
the base of Mount Tombstone.

Mountain. There wasn't a cloud in the sky, and just in case that changed we got what we could while we could.

The beauty of the land left us breathless. A continuous carpet of red and yellow sprawled across the valley, pinned at the corners by the weight of distant lakes, and walled by granite spires cutting into the blue sky above us. It would take us four days to hike back to the van. Four days of the most miraculous scenery of the trip. Our only worry was having enough film with us — our only worry, that is, apart from the bears.

Sarah and I awoke the first night with a start. We held our breath and strained our ears. A snort came from just outside the tent. God help us, we could hear a bear. It's a camper's worst nightmare. We'd heard reports of a sow and cub just one valley over and although we had a bottle of pepper spray with us, another story of a grizzly "eating it like candy" as two German tourists emptied their can ran through my mind. Our hearts began to pound. The snorts intensified. It seemed as if the bear was rooting into our gear. We froze, scared stiff. It was only feet away.

Wait a minute! Suddenly the snort took on a slightly different pitch, and what at first sounded like a hungry bear now sounded suspiciously like Pat snoring in his sleep. We let out our breath, buried ourselves in our sleeping bags and tried in vain to get back to sleep.

We soon found our prayers for light had been answered. Over the next four days not a single cloud broke the sheet of blue over our heads. It was clear to a fault. Without the diffusing effect of clouds, daylight was harsh and sunrise and sunset came and went quickly. Still, those next four days became the highlight of our trip. Backpacking in open tundra and along mountain ridges at the peak of fall colour, with Pat and Baiba as our guides, was more than we could have hoped for from the Yukon. The views were indescribable. Traversing ridge after ridge in the high arctic air kept reminding me of the monastery analogy. After months of travelling the country we had arrived at the summit, speechless.

Yet even these remote mountain passes were not exempt from development. Mineral exploration threatened the entire region. The truth is, there wasn't a place in the country Sarah and I could have gone where there weren't environmental difficulties, because we were part of the problem. As members of the human race we brought them with us. The problems originate with how we live, how we perceive the world. As a group, we consider nature a collection of subjects or a reservoir of utilities —

Frequent rainbows were a welcome effect of
the unpredictable mountain weather.

something separate and removed from ourselves. Perception has been polluted with a Midas touch.

Increasingly, I felt that my own photography was a way of stating that the landscape starts with ourselves. It is not something independent of us, it is us. A landscape photograph isn't devoid of people. A person composed it and other people will react to it. The pictures became statements of ownership. Not of the land, but of how we saw ourselves in it.

The last morning of our adventure found us on a mountain ridge so high that only a few handfuls of snow were available for our day's supply of water. We waited for sunrise to break across the lines of peaks that stretched around us. Those photographs we took then were symbolic of what we'd learned: that we create the world, our experience of the world, after our own image. Restoring nature to wholeness can only be accomplished by restoring ourselves to wholeness. The mountains and the threats they faced were a reflection of us, of our own challenges, our own possibilities.

HOPE

Clayoquot Sound

We started our journey across the country in a little-known corner of the east coast, observing how a small community deals with the ecological problems it faces. We ended our journey on the other side of the country in a place known internationally for how an ecological problem was faced there. Clayoquot Sound.

The events in Clayoquot Sound in the summer of 1993 have become legendary in the environmental movement. Books have been written and documentaries filmed about the drama and success of the blockades that were formed to stop clearcut logging within its old-growth forests. The rebellion has become part of the Canadian fabric and marks a turning point in our dealings with nature.

Everything about Clayoquot Sound is mythic. Massive whales roam the inlets. Titanic trees thick with sound-deadening moss cloak the mountains. Ethereal fogs and mists ebb between shore and sea. It is a place of gigantism, a botanical wonderland.

Dutch runs the Meares Island ferry, a one-man operation that boats tourists out to Meares Island Tribal Park. He had all the trimmings of an old sea captain: grizzled white beard, gold earrings, and a low "arrrgh, arrrgh" as he brought us ashore with his mooring pole.

Along the west coast of Vancouver Island stretch 170 watersheds and three large islands; a dozen of the watersheds and two of the islands are considered to be pristine. Six of these virgin watersheds and both islands can be found in Clayoquot Sound. Occupying over 260 000 hectares, Clayoquot Sound is home to the largest expanse of ancient rainforest remaining in North America, and home to bears, elk, wolves, cougars, bald eagles, ravens, song- and waterbirds, and several salmon species. Four of the watersheds, rich in salmon streams and with trees 1500 years old and up to 4.5 metres in girth, have been slated for logging.

Ocean fog enshrouds the rainforest at sunset.

We unloaded our gear and bid him ahoy. He'd be returning in three days, time enough for us to explore the rainforest, which quickly lived up to its name as the mist coalesced into larger and larger droplets.

Adrian Dorst, a well-known local photographer, had told us about Meares Island. We needed to photograph big trees and Meares had them in scores. We met him at his home just outside of Tofino and went through maps together, finding other suitable locations. It was then we realized, looking at the topography of the Sound, that trans-portation was going to be a problem. Our Zodiac would have been perfect — if only the motor hadn't blown in Quebec.

As the sound of Dutch's outboard faded into the distance we got our bearings.

Clayoquot Sound has been home for over 5000 years to many Aboriginal peoples including the Ahousaht, Hesquiaht and Tla-o-qui-aht First Nations. Native people make up almost half the Clayoquot Sound population, yet they only hold rights to one-half of 0.1 percent of the land. For several years the First Nations have been a dominant force behind the fight to protect what remains of the old-growth rainforests. For them, the banning of clearcut logging is not just an environmental issue but also one of human rights. For generations they have lived among the rainforests practising a traditional way of life with little impact on the land.

Meares Island, one of the two pristine islands in Clayoquot Sound and home to many Native people, was in the forefront of the logging debate. Macmillan Bloedel held logging rights to Meares Island, and in the early 1980s began making plans to log there. In 1985 the Tla-o-qui-aht First Nation announced the creation of a tribal park on Meares Island. The traditional societies banded together to form the Nuu-chah-nulth Tribal Council and won an appeal to temporarily prohibit logging on Meares until after their land claim case. The issue is still unresolved, but although Meares Island is not legally a tribal park, the island has escaped with minimal logging activity.

Leaving our packs, we took a short hike to get a sense of the island. It was our first experience in the rainforest and we needed a few moments to take it in before we began the search for a campsite.

Leaves crowding the edge of the trail clung to our limbs as we passed, streaking us with rainwater, while a thick drapery of moss, blurring the boundary between tree and forest floor, released heavy globules from above, gradually soaking us. The rain here

A vine grows in the cavity of gnarled driftwood.

doesn't fall from the sky; the canopy shuts out the sky completely. The forest is a world unto itself.

We walked a handmade trail of timber on a tour of the island's most remarkable trees. The cedars are celebrities, monoliths eighteen metres around with huge roots and crowns towering out of sight. The trail terminates at the "Hanging Garden Tree," so named because of the saplings, mosses and grasses that have taken root in the folds of its bark. The 2000-year-old tree has become its own ecosystem, a microcosm of the forest around. Indeed, every part of the forest seems to reflect a scaled version of the whole. We walked slowly among the trees, conscious of not wanting to intrude on the forest.

Very shortly we began to understand what the protests a few years before had been about. Clayoquot Valley is the largest low-elevation coastal rainforest on the planet. But these forests inspire much more than cerebral concern. It was a feeling that had followed us across the country. It was by the firepit in Glooscap, on the dunes of the Sandhills, under the mountains at sunrise. It originated with the landscape and was more than an appreciation of beauty. There was a sense that all the myriad parts of nature spoke with a single voice. It's a feeling that every lover of nature knows intuitively. Perhaps there are two types of people, those who seek to change nature, and those who seek to be changed by it.

Invigorated by the sights, we returned to our packs to begin our hike in earnest, taking a different, muddy trail close to the shoreline. Unfortunately, it didn't take long for the dense tangle of the rainforest and the slippery conditions to deteriorate both the trail and our spirits. The excursion had been a snap decision and, unable to find the proper dried foods in town, we had to resort to canned goods. Only an hour into

Clayoquot Sound, the mecca of Canadian environmentalism, was a fitting end to our journey.

In 1993, protesters staged the largest civil disobedience operation in Canadian history. An estimated 12 000 individuals from all sectors of the community and abroad attended a peace camp, organizing blockades and protests against the provincial government's decision to clear-cut almost three-quarters of Clayoquot Sound. Over 850 people, some from as far away as Europe and Australia, were arrested on the grounds of defying a Supreme Court order prohibiting public interference with Macmillan Bloedel's cutting operations.

have to do it in half the time, was nearly more than we could take. We promised ourselves a hotel room as incentive.

Dutch, returning with another load of tourists, was as surprised to see us as we were embarrassed to see him. Three hours in the rainforest had transformed us into a couple of soggy dishrags.

Still nursing bruises from awkwardly packed Ravioli, we chose a more leisurely hike along one of Clayoquot's many beaches. At low tide the saturated sand reflects the sky with a silver sheen, creating the illusion of walking on water. We searched for starfish and anemones among the rocky outcrops and spent hours huddled over tide pools, marvelling, like children exploring puddles. It was one of the most relaxing and restoring times of our trip. We lay in the soft sand, taking in the mountain vistas, while a briny wind carried in the fresh scents of the ocean. Lulled by the sound of surf echoing around us, we planned our next adventure, a whale-watching expedition.

Perhaps the best way to describe whale breath is a literal one: it is the smell of two

After all our experiences, including the disheartening ones, we felt optimistic, even excited, and invigorated by the challenges.

tonnes of partly digested fish. And it is one drawback to a close encounter with these amazing animals.

Our first trip was unsuccessful. A sunset cruise with a local operator was frustrated by evening fog. The next day we got luckier. Far out in the middle of Clayoquot Sound we came upon three feeding grey whales. Our Native guide had an amazing intuitive knowledge of where they would surface. Noticing my camera, he invited me up to the helm for personal instructions on their movement.

On the trip back to port, the first mate, the captain's son, told us about the area. Between stories of eagles snatching cats from town and kayakers being hit by tankers, he pointed to an opening between two distant mountain ridges.

"See there? You can just see the clear-cutting in the distance," he said, turning back

---

Since 1993 over 350 000 cubic metres of lumber have been harvested in Clayoquot Sound. However, over the last ten years, the volume of wood logged in the area has been on a steady decline, from almost one million cubic metres in 1988 to 77 000 cubic metres in 1997 and none in 1998. In 1999, no trees had been cut in Clayoquot Sound as of August.

In 1997, MacMillan Bloedel formed a Joint Venture Corporation (JVC) with the Nuu-chah-nulth First Nations called Iisaak Forest Resources (of which the First Nations own 51 percent). In June 1999, Iisaak signed a Memorandum of Under-standing (MOU) along with four environmental organizations in an agreement not to harvest Clayoquot Sound's virgin watersheds in Iisaak's tenure, and to begin phasing out the logging of old-growth timber completely. Interfor, another Clayoquot logging company, did not sign the agreement, leaving pristine watersheds in their tenure vulnerable. Shortly after the signing of the MOU, MacMillan Bloedel accepted a proposed offer to buy the company by American-based Weyerhaeuser, which has agreed to continue the JVC with First Nations and to follow through with the MOU.

to us. "The logging companies won't go where the tourists can see them. But every-where else..." his voice trailed off.

What Sarah and I initially imagined as a "last chance to see" journey turned into our first chance at really seeing, at understanding. The environment can't be preserved with more business as usual, that's clear. But neither does it have to be a tormenting purge or sacrifice. It's merely a refocusing, an awakening to the implications, the pos-itive implications of how we live our life. The publicity on both sides of the environ-mental front is misleading. We should neither be scared into action, nor lulled into inaction. There is a gift in the coming environmental changes we must make. The gift of meaning.

Ultimately, our travels across the country were not discouraging, but empowering. Feeling a sense of loss turned out to be the first step to feeling hope, because we learned how much we, and others like us, cared. Looking forward to our uncertain future, this balance of loss and care provides a cautious optimism. We are ready to believe in change. Ready to care before it is lost.

BIBLIOGRAPHY

Austin-Smith Jr., Peter. August 1995. *Hampton-Kennebecasis Marsh Complex: Management Plan*.

Austin-Smith Jr., Peter. September 1994. *Hampton-Kennebecasis Marsh Complex: Status Report*.

Banff—Bow Valley Study. 1996. *Banff—Bow Valley: At the Crossroads*. Summary Report of the Banff—Bow Valley Task Force (Robert Page, Suzanne Bayley, J. Douglas Cook, Jeffrey E. Green, and J.R. Brent Ritchie). Prep. for the Honourable Sheila Copps, Minister of Canadian Heritage, Ottawa, Ontario.

Berry, Thomas. 1988. *The Dream of the Earth*. Sierra Club Books. San Francisco.

Canada. Dominion Bureau of Statistics. 1997. *Canada Year Book*. Ottawa: Statistics Canada.

Canada. Dominion Bureau of Statistics. 1999. *Canada Year Book*. Ottawa: Statistics Canada.

Cheeseman, Tim (MCIP). May 5, 1994. *Great Sand Hills Planning District: Development Plan*. Rural Municipality of Clinworth No. 230, Bylaw No. 5-94.

Cheeseman, Tim (MCIP). June 16, 1994. *Great Sand Hills*. Rural Municipality of Clinworth No. 230, Zoning Bylaw No. 6-94.

Cundiff, Brad. Fall 1993. Carolinian Canada. *Borealis*. 14:17—22.

Department of Environment, Nova Scotia. May 8, 1991. *Environmental Assessment Report: Final Guidelines for the Preparation of Terms of Reference*. Kelly Rock Limited. Kelly's Mountain Aggregate Quarry.

Friends of Clayoquot Sound. Newsletters. Summer 1993—Spring 1996; Spring 1999.

Friends of Clayoquot Sound. July 28, 1999. Temperate Rainforest Fact Sheet and Clayoquot Sound Update.

Gorrie, Peter. 1994. The Enchanted Woodland. *Canadian Geographic*. Vol. 114, No. 2, pp. 32—42.

Hills, Stewart. 1985. Private Stewardship. *Seasons*. Vol. 25, No. 2.

Identification Committee of Carolinian Canada, The. 1985. *Critical Unprotected Areas in the Carolinian Life Zone of Canada: Final Report*. Nature Conservancy of Canada, The Ontario Heritage Foundation, WWF Canada.

Jacques, Elane. 1985. The Landowner Contract Project. *Seasons*. Vol. 25, No. 2.

Keating, Michael and the Canadian Global Change Program. 1997. *Canada and the State of the Planet: The social, economic and environmental trends that are shaping our lives*. Oxford University Press. Toronto.

Lompart, Chris. 1995. Temagami: Five Lost Years. *Seasons*. Vol. 35, No. 3.

Love, David. 1985. Creatures in Peril. *Seasons*. Vol. 25, No. 2.

Marty, Sid. 1997. Homeless on the Range: Grizzlies Struggle for Elbow Room and Survival in Banff National Park. *Canadian Geographic*. Vol. 117, No. 1, pp. 28—39.

McNamee, Kevin. 1994. *The National Parks of Canada*. Key Porter Books. Toronto.

National Wetlands Working Group. 1988. *Wetlands of Canada*. Ecological Land Classification Series, No. 24. Sustainable Development Branch, Environment Canada, Ottawa, Ontario and Polyscience Publications Inc., Montreal, Quebec.

Ontario Legislative Assembly. Standing Committee on Resources Development. 1989. *Resource Management in the Temagami Area*. Toronto.

Poling, Tim. 1996. Temagami: Logging plan fires environmentalists. *Ontario Out of Doors*. Vol. 28, No. 7.

Price, Steven. 1985. The Carolinian Canada Conservation Strategy. *Seasons*. Vol. 25, No. 2.

Quinby, Peter A. 1996. *Ancient Forest Exploration and Research*. Scientist's Report. Action Alert.

Regully, Bob. Summer 1996. Not So Great Lakes. *Outdoor Canada*. pp. 39—48.

Reid, Ron. 1985. Exploring Canada's Deep South. *Seasons*. Vol. 25, No. 2.

Reid, Ron et al. September 1996. *Towards a Conservation Strategy for Carolinian Canada: Issues and Options*.

Robertson, Marion. 1969. *Red Earth: Tales of the Micmacs*. Nova Scotia Museum. Halifax, Nova Scotia.

Saskatchewan Environment and Public Safety. May 1991. *Great Sand Hills Land Use Strategy*. Saskatchewan.

Smith, Robert Leo. 1992. *Elements of Ecology*. Third edition. Harper Collins. New York.

Western Canada Wilderness Committee. Summer 1985. *Meares Island News*. Vancouver, BC.

Western Canada Wilderness Committee. 1995. Protect Ursus Valley, *Ahousaht Territory*, Vol. 14, No. 2.

Western Canada Wilderness Committee. 1996. *Beautiful Clayoquot Sound*. Vol. 15, No. 12.

Wildlands League, et al. 1996. *Temagami: Act Now! Action Bulletin*.

World Wildlife Fund. Endangered Spaces Campaign 95—96. *Yukon and the Endangered Spaces Campaign*.

Yukon Conservation Society and Canadian Parks and Wilderness Society—Yukon Chapter. *Yukon Wild: Natural Regions of the Yukon*.

SUGGESTED READING

Carrol, John E., et al. 1997. *The Greening of Faith: God, the Environment, and the Good Life*. University Press of New England. Hanover, NH.

Carson, Rachel. 1962. *Silent Spring*. Houghton Mifflin Company. New York.

Ehrlich, Paul R and Anne H. Ehrlich. 1991. *Healing the Planet: Strategies for Resolving the Environmental Crisis*. Addison-Wesley. Reading, MA.

Gottlieb, Roger S. 1996. *This Sacred Earth: Religion, Nature, Environment*. Routledge. New York.

Hartmann, Thom. 1998. *The Last Hours of Ancient Sunlight*. Mythical Books. Northfield, VT.

Leopold, Aldo. 1949. *A Sand County Almanac*. Oxford University Press. New York.

Sessions, George. 1995. *Deep Ecology for the 21st Century: Readings on the Philosophy and Practice of the New Environmentalism*. Shambhala Publications. Boston.

Snyder, Gary. 1995. *A Place In Space: Ethics, Aesthetics, and Watersheds*. Counterpoint. Washington, DC.

Suzuki, David. 1994. *Time To Change*. Stoddart. Toronto.

Suzuki, David. 1997. *The Sacred Balance*. Greystone Books. Vancouver, BC.

Swimme, Brian. 1984. *The Universe is a Green Dragon: A Cosmic Creation Story*. Bear & Company Publishing. Santa Fe.

Wilson, Edward O. 1992. *The Diversity of Life*. The Belknap Press of Harvard University. Cambridge, MA.

Zimmerman, Michael E. 1994. *Contesting Earth's Future: Radical Ecology and Postmodernity*. University of California Press. Berkeley.

RELATED ORGANIZATIONS

Canada Centre for Inland Waters: www.CCIW.ca

Canadian Nature Federation: 1 Nicholas Street, Suite 520, Ottawa, ON K1N 7B7;
   Telephone: 613-562-3447; Fax: 613-562-3371.

Canadian Parks and Wilderness Society (CPAWS): 880 Wellington Street, Suite 506, Ottawa, ON
   K1R 6K7; info@cpaws.org; webmaster@cpaws.org

Carolinian Canada: 659 Exeter Road, London, ON N6E 1L3; info@carolinian.org

Earthroots: 401 Richmond Street West, Suite 410, Toronto, ON M5V 3A8; Telephone: 416-599-0152;
   Fax: 416-340-2429; eroot@web.net

Friends of Clayoquot Sound: Box 489, Tofino, BC V0R 2Z0; Telephone: 250-725-4218;
   Fax: 250-725-2527; www.island.net/~focs/index.htm

Friends of Temagami: P.O. Box 398, Temagami, ON P0H 2H0; Telephone: 705-569-3539;
   Fax: 705-569-2710.

Greenpeace: 185 Spadina Avenue, 6th Floor, Toronto, ON M5T 2C5; Telephone: 416-597-8408;
   Fax: 416-597-8422.

Hampton Area Environment Group: Judy Maddox, secretary; Telephone: 506-832-4251.

Micmac Historical Cultural Arts Society: http://personal.nbnet.ca/cdedam/links.html

Nature Conservancy of Canada: 110 Eglinton Avenue West, 4th Floor, Toronto, ON M4R 2G5;
   Telephone: 416-932-3202; Fax: 416-932-3208.

Sierra Club: 517 College Street, Suite 204, Toronto, ON M6G 4A2; Telephone: 416-960-9606;
   Fax: 416-960-0020.

Township of Temagami: www.twp.temagami.on.ca

Western Canada Wilderness Committee: 20 Water Street, Vancouver, BC V6B 1A4;
   Telephone: 604-683-8220; Fax: 604-683-8229; www.web.net/wewild/welcome

World Wildlife Fund Canada, 245 Eglinton Avenue East, Suite 410, Toronto, ON M4P 3J1;
   Telephone: 416-489-8800; 1-800-26-PANDA; Fax: 416-489-3611; www.wwfcanada.org

Yukon Conservation Society: Box 4163, Whitehorse, YT Y1A 3T3; Telephone: 403-668-5678;
   Fax: 403-668-6637

Index

Page numbers in bold refer to photographs.